Activities Manual for MICROPROCESSORS Principles and Applications

Charles M. Gilmore
The Heath Company
Benton Harbor, Michigan

GLENCOE/McGRAW-HILL

A Macmillan/McGraw-Hill Company

Mission Hills, California ■ New York, New York

ACKNOWLEDGMENTS

The *Basic Skills in Electricity and Electronics* series was conceived and developed through the talents and energies of many individuals and organizations.

The original, on-site classroom testing of the texts and manuals in this series was conducted at the Burr D. Coe Vocational Technical High School, East Brunswick, New Jersey; Chantilly Secondary School, Chantilly, Virginia; Nashoba Valley Technical High School, Westford, Massachusetts; Platt Regional Vocational Technical High School, Milford, Connecticut; and the Edgar Thomson, Irvin Works of the United States Steel Corporation, Dravosburg, Pennsylvania. Postpublication testing took place at the Alhambra High School, Phoenix, Arizona; St. Helena High School, St. Helena, California; and Addison Trail High School, Addison, Illinois.

Early in the publication life of this series, the appellation "Rainbow Books" was used. The name stuck and has become a point of identification ever since.

In the years since the publication of this series, extensive follow-up studies and research have been conducted. Thousands of instructors, students, school administrators, and industrial trainers have shared their experiences and suggestions with the authors and publishers. To each of these people we extend our thanks and appreciation.

Activities Manual for Microprocessors: Principles and Applications

Send all inquiries to:
Glencoe/McGraw-Hill
936 Eastwind Drive
Westerville, Ohio 43081

ISBN 0-07-023412-4

1 2 3 4 5 6 7 8 9 0 MALMAL 9 8 7 6 5 4 3 2 1 0

Contents

Editor's Foreword

The McGraw-Hill *Basic Skills in Electricity and Electronics* series has been designed to provide entry-level competencies in a wide range of occupations in the electric and electronic fields. The series consists of coordinated instructional materials designed especially for the career-oriented student. Each major subject area covered in the series is supported by a textbook, an activities manual, and a teacher's manual. All the materials focus on the theory, practices, applications, and experiences necessary for those preparing to enter technical careers.

There are two fundamental considerations in the preparation of materials for such a series: the needs of the learner and the needs of the employer. The materials in this series meet these needs in an expert fashion. The authors and editors have drawn upon their broad teaching and technical experiences to accurately interpret and meet the needs of the student. The needs of business and industry have been identified through questionnaires, surveys, personal interviews, industry publications, government occupational trend reports, and field studies.

The processes used to produce and refine the series have been ongoing. Technological change is rapid and the content has been revised to focus on current trends. Refinements in pedagogy have been defined and implemented based on classroom testing and feedback from students and teachers using the series. Every effort has been made to offer the best possible learning materials.

The widespread acceptance of the *Basic Skills in Electricity and Electronics* series and the positive responses from users confirm the basic soundness in the content and design of these materials as well as their effectiveness as learning tools. Teachers will find the texts and manuals in each of the subject areas logically structured, well-paced, and developed around a framework of modern objectives. Students will find the materials readable, lucidly illustrated, and interesting. They will also find a generous amount of self-study and review materials to help them determine their own progress.

The publisher and editor welcome comments and suggestions from teachers and students using the materials in this series.

Charles A. Schuler
Project Editor

BASIC SKILLS IN ELECTRICITY AND ELECTRONICS
Charles A. Schuler, Project Editor

Books in this series:

Introduction to Television Servicing by Wayne C. Brandenberg
Electricity: Principles and Applications by Richard J. Fowler
Communication Electronics by Louis E. Frenzel, Jr.
Instruments and Measurements by Charles M. Gilmore
Microprocessors: Principles and Applications by Charles M. Gilmore
Small Appliance Repair by Phyllis Palmore and Nevin E. André
Electronics: Principles and Applications by Charles A. Schuler
Digital Electronics by Roger L. Tokheim

Preface

This activities manual has been designed to accompany the text *Microprocessors: Principles and Applications*. A total of thirty-eight activities are presented. Included are tests for each chapter of the text, along with various research and experimental activities.

Most of the chapter tests consist of multiple-choice questions. However, several chapter tests also include short-answer essay-type questions as well. The tests contain enough multiple-choice and essay questions so that the instructor can pick and choose questions that are most pertinent, while skipping over the others.

The experiments that use a microprocessor trainer or breadboard are oriented toward 6800-family trainers, such as the Heath 6400-series units. In a few experiments, a microcomputer is required. An MS-DOS, 8088-based machine is specified for use here. A simple single-floppy disk unit with 256K RAM and a monochrome display will suffice for these applications. The 6400-series trainer and the MS-DOS microcomputer were chosen because of their wide availability and relatively low cost.

Microprocessors are not simple devices, and naturally, neither are microprocessor-based systems. With this in mind, this activities manual gradually introduces the microprocessor to the student. This allows the student a reasonable amount of time to become comfortable with the fundamentals of microprocessor instruction sets, programming, hardware, and applications.

The author wishes to thank Denton J. Dailey for his assistance in the preparation of this manual.

Charles M. Gilmore

Safety

Electric and electronic circuits can be dangerous. Safe practices are necessary to prevent electrical shock, fires, explosions, mechanical damage, and injuries resulting from the improper use of tools.

Perhaps the greatest hazard is electrical shock. A current through the human body in excess of 10 milliamperes can paralyze the victim and make it impossible to let go of a "live" conductor or component. Ten milliamperes is a rather small amount of electric flow: it is only *ten one-thousandths* of an ampere. An ordinary flashlight uses more than 100 times that amount of current!

Flashlight cells and batteries are safe to handle because the resistance of human skin is normally high enough to keep the current flow very small. For example, touching an ordinary 1.5-V cell produces a current flow in the microampere range (a microampere is one-millionth of an ampere). This much current is too small to be noticed.

High voltage, on the other hand, can force enough current through the skin to produce a shock. If the current approaches 100 milliamperes or more, the shock can be fatal. Thus, the danger of shock increases with voltage. Those who work with high voltage must be properly trained and equipped.

When human skin is moist or cut, its resistance to the flow of electricity can drop drastically. When this happens, even moderate voltages may cause a serious shock. Experienced technicians know this and they also know that so-called low-voltage equipment may have a high-voltage section or two. In other words, they do not practice two methods of working with circuits: one for high voltage and one for low voltage. They follow safe procedures at all times. They do not assume protective devices are working. They do not assume a circuit is off even though the switch is in the OFF position. They know the switch could be defective.

As your knowledge and experience grow, you will learn many specific safe procedures for dealing with electricity and electronics. In the meantime:

1. Always follow procedures.
2. Use service manuals as often as possible. They often contain specific safety information.
3. Investigate before you act.
4. When in doubt, *do not act*. Ask your instructor or supervisor.

GENERAL SAFETY RULES FOR ELECTRICITY AND ELECTRONICS

Safe practices will protect you and your fellow workers. Study the following rules. Discuss them with others, and ask your instructor about any that you do not understand.

1. Do not work when you are tired or taking medicine that makes you drowsy.
2. Do not work in poor light.
3. Do not work in damp areas or with wet shoes or clothing.
4. Use approved tools, equipment, and protective devices.
5. Avoid wearing rings, bracelets, and similar metal items when working around exposed electric circuits.
6. Never assume that a circuit is off. Double check it with an instrument that you are sure is operational.
7. Some situations require a "buddy system" to guarantee that power will not be turned on while a technician is still working on a circuit.
8. Never tamper with or try to override safety devices such as an interlock (a type of switch that automatically removes power when a door is opened or a panel removed).
9. Keep tools and test equipment clean and in good working condition. Replace insulated probes and leads at the first sign of deterioration.
10. Some devices, such as capacitors, can store a *lethal* charge. They may store this charge for long periods of time. You must be certain these devices are discharged before working around them.
11. Do not remove grounds, and do not use adaptors that defeat the equipment ground.
12. Use only an approved fire extinguisher for electric and electronic equipment. Water can conduct electricity and may severely damage equipment. Carbon dioxide (CO_2) or halogenated-type extinguishers are usually preferred. Foam-type extinguishers may also be desired in some cases. Commercial fire extinguishers are rated for the type of fires for which they are effective. Use only those rated for the proper working conditions.
13. Follow directions when using solvents and other chemicals. They may be toxic, flammable, or may damage certain materials such as plastics.
14. A few materials used in electronic equipment are toxic. Examples include tantalum capacitors and beryllium oxide transistor cases. These devices should not be crushed or abraded, and you should wash your hands thoroughly after handling them. Other materials (such as heat shrink tubing) may produce irritating fumes if overheated.

15. Certain circuit components affect the safe performance of equipment and systems. Use only exact or approved replacement parts.

16. Use protective clothing and safety glasses when handling high-vacuum devices such as picture tubes and cathode ray tubes.

17. Don't work on equipment before you know proper procedures and are aware of any potential safety hazards.

18. Many accidents have been caused by people rushing and cutting corners. Take the time required to protect yourself and others. Running, horseplay, and practical jokes are strictly forbidden in shops and laboratories. Circuits and equipment must be treated with respect. Learn how they work and the proper way of working on them. Always practice safety; your health and life depend on it.

CHAPTER | 1

What Is the Microprocessor?

ACTIVITY 1-1
TEST: WHAT IS
THE MICROPROCESSOR?

For questions 1 to 9, on a separate sheet of paper, determine whether each statement is true or false.

1. Microprocessors were developed during World War II.
2. Microcomputers are considered general-purpose devices.
3. The term "architecture" refers to the type of software that a microcomputer will run.
4. The term "bit" stands for binary digit.
5. A common microcomputer output device is the CRT.
6. A single BCD digit requires 4 bits for representation.
7. The ALU is the section of the microcomputer where data and program instructions are stored.
8. A byte may be defined as being 4 or 8 bits in length, depending on the microprocessor being studied.
9. Microcomputers and computers in general operate on what is called the stored-program concept.

For questions 10 to 20, choose the letter that best completes each statement.

10. Microprocessors are examples of _____.
    a. Linear integrated circuits
    b. Large-scale integrated circuits
    c. Data storage devices
    d. Random-access memory

11. Alphanumeric input is usually provided by _____.
    a. A microcomputer bus
    b. Read-only memory
    c. Floppy disk drives
    d. A keyboard

12. The circuit boards that are placed in a microcomputer are usually connected together by _____.
    a. Ribbon cables
    b. Optical fibers
    c. A bus
    d. Very strong wood glue

13. A common measure of the relative power of a microprocessor is _____.
   - *a.* The number of lines in the address bus
   - *b.* The number of lines in the data bus
   - *c.* The clock speed
   - *d.* All of the above

14. The microprocessor data bus _____.
   - *a.* Carries instruction addresses to memory
   - *b.* Carries addresses to input and output devices
   - *c.* Is used to transfer data to and from the CPU
   - *d.* All of the above

15. A benchmark program is used to _____.
   - *a.* Process analog signals
   - *b.* Measure the size of the address bus
   - *c.* Compare relative speeds of microprocessors
   - *d.* Provide an interface between the computer and the CRT

16. The microprocessor's control circuits are used to fetch and execute _____.
   - *a.* Data
   - *b.* ALU
   - *c.* MPU
   - *d.* Program instructions

17. Most of the first 16-bit microprocessor designs were taken from _____.
   - *a.* Calculators
   - *b.* 8-bit microprocessors
   - *c.* Microcomputers
   - *d.* TTL SSI

18. Typically, an 8-bit microprocessor can address how many memory locations? _____.
   - *a.* 16K
   - *b.* 32K
   - *c.* 64K
   - *d.* 128K

19. When computer architecture and LSI techniques are brought together, you have _____.
   - *a.* SSI, MSI, and LSI
   - *b.* Memory ICs
   - *c.* A microprocessor
   - *d.* All of the above

20. This development was responsible for the production of smaller computers: _____.
   - *a.* Color television
   - *b.* Integrated circuits
   - *c.* Vacuum tubes
   - *d.* Multitronic units

ACTIVITY 1-2
RESEARCH

PURPOSE

In this activity you will determine basic information regarding the microprocessor and microcomputer equipment available for laboratory use.

MATERIALS

Microprocessor trainer, microcomputer, operations manuals and literature.

PROCEDURE

Determine the following information about the microprocessor and/or microcomputer equipment that you will be using. If microcomputers are not going to be used, then leave the MICROCOMPUTER column blank.

	Microprocessor Trainer	Microcomputer
Manufacturer	_____	_____
CPU type	_____	_____
Data bus width	_____	_____
Address bus width	_____	_____
Clock frequency	_____	_____
Max. memory	_____	_____
Memory present (RAM)	_____	_____

CHAPTER | 2

The Decimal and Binary Number Systems

ACTIVITY 2-1
TEST: THE DECIMAL
AND BINARY NUMBER SYSTEMS

On a separate piece of paper, choose the letter that best completes each of the following statements.

1. The radix of a number system is _____.
   a. The number of symbols used to represent numbers in a number system
   b. Used to determine the positional weight of a digit
   c. Another name for the base of a number system
   d. All of the above

2. Binary and hexadecimal codes are _____.
   a. Examples of alphanumeric codes
   b. Less efficient than BCD in expressing numbers
   c. Positionally weighted codes
   d. All of the above

3. The radix point _____.
   a. Separates positive and negative numbers
   b. Separates the fractional and integer parts of a number
   c. Is used only in base-10 arithmetic
   d. Is placed beside the MSB of a binary number

4. The most significant bit of an 8-bit number _____.
   a. Has a decimal weight of 128
   b. Will always be equal to 1
   c. Is located to the right of the binary point
   d. Has a decimal weight of 127

5. A mixed number _____.
   a. Contains binary and decimal system symbols
   b. Is an example of an integer
   c. Has a value of less than 1
   d. Has a whole number part and a fractional part

6. An integer is _____.
   a. A positive number
   b. A fraction

c. A nonterminating binary fraction

d. A positive or negative whole number

7. How many different decimal numbers can be represented by a three-digit octal number? _____

    a. 512   *c.* 2048

    b. 1024   *d.* 4096

8. How many binary bits are required to represent FFF_{16} different numbers? _____

    a. 4   *c.* 12

    b. 8   *d.* 16

9. How many decimal numbers can be represented by a four-digit hex number? _____

    a. 2^{16} *c.* 65.536K

    b. 65.536×10^3 *d.* All of the above

10. The decimal fraction 0.4_{10} _____.

    a. Is a whole number

    b. Represents a repeating, nonterminating binary fraction equivalent

    c. Has an exact binary fraction equivalent

    d. Has no binary fractional equivalent

11. Copy Table 2-1 and perform the necessary conversions.

Table 2-1

	Decimal	Octal	Binary	Hex		Decimal	Octal	Binary	Hex
a.	15				n.		12		
b.			1101		o.			1010 0110	
c.				E	p.		271		
d.		37			q.	27			
e.			11100		r.		377		
f.				10	s.				F8
g.	41				t.			0011	
h.			1110 0001		u.	19			
i.				5	v.		22		
j.	17				w.			11	
k.		176			x.				14
l.				EA	y.		134		
m.	102				z.				38

Table 2-2

	Decimal	Octal	Binary	Hex		Decimal	Octal	Binary	Hex
a.	25.25				g.			11.1	
b.		17.1			h.	10.0625			
c.			11.011		i.		25.02		
d.				5.C	j.			1001.001	
e.	27.125				k.				011.1
f.		1.7							

12. Copy Table 2-2 and perform the necessary conversions.

ACTIVITY 2-2
LAB EXPERIMENT:
NUMBER BASE CONVERSIONS

PURPOSE

This activity will accomplish two objectives. First, you will learn how to load, review, correct, and execute a program on your microprocessor trainer. Second, you will become familiar with making binary-to-decimal and decimal-to-binary conversions.

MATERIALS

Qty.
1   Microprocessor trainer
2   Program listings

INTRODUCTION

In this activity you will convert binary numbers into decimal numbers and decimal numbers into binary numbers. The easiest way to convert binary numbers into decimal numbers is to add the decimal weights assigned to each column. For a 16-bit number, the weights are assigned as shown in Fig. 2-1. For example, to convert the binary number $1100\ 1010_2$ to decimal, we add the positional weights as shown in Fig. 2-2. In this case, we find $1100\ 1010_2 = 202_{10}$.

MSB
↓

Weight	2^{15}	2^{14}	2^{13}	2^{12}	2^{11}	2^{10}	2^9	2^8	2^7	2^6	2^5	2^4	2^3	2^2	2^1	2^0
Bit	15	14	13	12	11	10	9	8	7	6	5	4	3	2	1	0

↑
LSB

Fig. 2-1

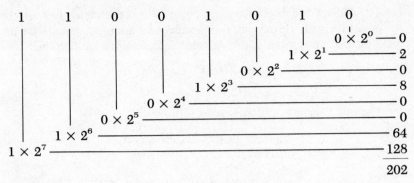

Fig. 2-2

To convert a decimal number into a binary number, we repeatedly divide the decimal number by 2. The remainder will be either 0 or 1. This first remainder is the LSB of the binary number. We continue division by 2 until the result (the quotient) is zero. The remainder of the last division is the MSB of the binary number. Figure 2-3 demonstrates the process whereby 202_{10} is converted into binary form.

PROCEDURE

Part 1

1. Your instructor will give you a program to load into your microprocessor trainer. It will be given in the following format.
   Address 0   Contents 0
   Address 1   Contents 1
   Address 2   Contents 2
   Address 3   Contents 3

Division	Remainder	
$2\overline{)202}$ 101	0	LSB
$2\overline{)101}$ 50	1	
$2\overline{)50}$ 25	0	
$2\overline{)25}$ 12	1	
$2\overline{)12}$ 6	0	
$2\overline{)6}$ 3	0	
$2\overline{)3}$ 1	1	
$2\overline{)1}$ 0	1	MSB

Therefore, $202_{10} = 1100\ 1010_2$

Fig. 2-3

The address and its contents will be given in hexadecimal (or possibly octal) form. For example, the hexadecimal address contents for an 8-bit microprocessor with 64K addressing might look like this:

Address (Hex)   Contents (Hex)
00A2   3D

The octal form would appear as follows.

Address (Octal)   Contents (Octal)
000–242   075

2. To load the program, you must first enter the starting address.
3. Once the starting address is entered, you can enter the contents that belong at that location.
4. Many microprocessor trainers/breadboards automatically increment to the next memory location after the preceding memory location's contents have been entered. If that is the case with your trainer, simply enter the contents of the next memory location. If your trainer does not increment automatically, you will have to address the next location before you enter the contents of the second location.
5. Once you have loaded the first two memory locations, you can continue by loading each memory location called for by the program listing. It is wise to check frequently to be sure that you are loading the correct contents into the correct memory location. It is very easy to skip a number or a location! The program will not run if even one digit is entered incorrectly. If you are using a trainer that displays hex numbers on seven-segment displays, be sure you do not confuse the number 6 with the letter b.
6. Once the program is loaded, you should examine each location to be sure that it has the correct contents. Most microprocessor trainers have a key that lets you step through successive memory locations and examine the contents of each.
7. Each error found in the loaded program must be corrected. You must enter the address where the contents are in error and key in the correct contents.
8. Once the program is correctly loaded, you can execute it. To do so, you must load the microprocessor's program counter with the program's starting address. Once that is done, you can start execution.
9. When the program is running, it will first display an 8-bit binary number. As soon as the number is displayed, enter it on a copy of Table 2-3. You should immediately convert the number to decimal form and write the decimal number on the line under the decimal heading on a copy of Table 2-3.
10. The object is to beat the microprocessor. It will hold the binary display for a while and then give you the decimal number. That gives you time to check the accuracy of your conversion.
11. Complete Table 2-3 by doing 25 binary-to-decimal conversions.

Part 2

1. Your instructor will give you a memory location and the new contents to load into that location. The smaller the number you put into the location, the faster the microprocessor will make the binary-to-decimal conversion.
2. Experiment with different values and see how quickly you can make conversions.

Table 2-3 Binary-to-Decimal Conversion

Random Number	Binary	Decimal
1		
2		
3		
4		
5		
6		
7		
8		
9		
10		
11		
12		
13		
14		
15		
16		
17		
18		
19		
20		
21		
22		
23		
24		
25		

Table 2-4 Decimal-to-Binary Conversion

Random Number	Decimal	Binary
1		
2		
3		
4		
5		
6		
7		
8		
9		
10		
11		
12		
13		
14		
15		
16		
17		
18		
19		
20		
21		
22		
23		
24		
25		

1. Load the decimal-to-binary program by using the same method you used to load the binary-to-decimal program.
2. Examine the program to be sure it was entered correctly.
3. Correct any loading errors.
4. Execute the program.
5. Enter the decimal numbers produced by the trainer and your binary responses in a copy of Table 2-4.
6. After you are comfortable converting from decimal to binary, you can speed up the program. Use lower numbers in the new address your instructor gives you for this program's speedup address.

ACTIVITY 2-3
LAB EXPERIMENT:
BINARY-TO-OCTAL CONVERSION

PURPOSE

This experiment is designed to improve your binary-to-octal and octal-to-binary conversion skills. It will also help you gain further familiarity with your microprocessor trainer.

MATERIALS

Qty.
1 Microprocessor trainer
2 Program listings

INTRODUCTION

Octal notation is based on the octal number system. It uses the eight characters 0 to 7, which represent the decimal values 0 to 7. We use octal notation with microprocessors because it is a good shorthand for expressing long binary numbers. Octal is used because $8 = 2^3$, which means that one octal digit can exactly represent all the possible combinations of three binary digits (bits). The relationship is:

Binary	Octal
000	0
001	1
010	2
011	3
100	4
101	5
110	6
111	7

To convert a binary number to octal, you group the binary digits by threes *starting* at the binary point. For example, 1011.1101_2 converts to 13.64_8:

001	011	.	110	100
1	3	.	6	4

Leading and trailing insignificant 0s are used to complete the groups of three.

For the 8-bit binary integer 1011 1101 we have:

010	111	101
2	7	5

Note that the maximum octal representation of an 8-bit number is 377. Often, 2-byte (16-bit) numbers are represented in *offset octal*. This just means that each byte is converted separately. Therefore, the range of offset octal numbers for a 16-bit number is $000-000_8$ to $377-377_8$.

Converting octal to binary is easily done by reversing the process. For example, the octal number 247 is:

2	4	7
10	100	111

in 8-bit binary. Note: The ninth (insignificant) 0 is not shown.

PROCEDURE

Part 1

1. Load the binary-to-octal program.
2. Examine the program to be sure it is correctly loaded.
3. Correct any errors.
4. Execute the program.
5. Record the binary numbers given by the microprocessor and your answers in a copy of Table 2-5.
6. When you feel comfortable with binary-to-octal conversion, ask your instructor for the speedup address.

Part 2

1. Load, verify, correct, and execute the octal-to-binary program.
2. Record the octal numbers and your binary answers in a copy of Table 2-6.
3. Again, obtain the speedup address from your instructor and see how quickly you can make the conversions.

ACTIVITY 2-4
LAB EXPERIMENT:
BINARY-TO-HEXADECIMAL
CONVERSION

PURPOSE

This activity is designed to test your binary-to-hexadecimal conversion skills. Note that, because hexadecimal is the notation most commonly used in microprocessor work, you will want to practice such conversions until you become really good at doing them.

MATERIALS

Qty.

1 Microprocessor trainer
2 Program listings

Table 2-5 Binary-to-Octal Conversion

Random Number	Binary	Octal
1		
2		
3		
4		
5		
6		
7		
8		
9		
10		
11		
12		
13		
14		
15		
16		
17		
18		
19		
20		
21		
22		
23		
24		
25		

Table 2-6 Octal-to-Binary Conversion

Random Number	Octal	Binary
1		
2		
3		
4		
5		
6		
7		
8		
9		
10		
11		
12		
13		
14		
15		
16		
17		
18		
19		
20		
21		
22		
23		
24		
25		

INTRODUCTION

Hexadecimal notation has the same purpose in microprocessor work as octal notation has. It is used as a shorthand for binary numbers.

Hexadecimal (base 16) is used because its 16 characters can represent the 16 possible combinations found in a 4-bit binary number. That is, $2^4 = 16$. The relationship is:

Binary	Hex	Binary	Hex
0000	0	1000	8
0001	1	1001	9
0010	2	1010	A
0011	3	1011	B
0100	4	1100	C
0101	5	1101	D
0110	6	1110	E
0111	7	1111	F

Converting from binary to hexadecimal is simple. You group the bits into fours *starting* at the binary point. For example, 1011.1101_2 converts to $B.D_{16}$:

$$1011 \quad . \quad 1101_2$$
$$B \quad . \quad D_{16}$$

and $1011\ 1101_2$ converts to BD_{16}.

To convert from hexadecimal to binary, you reverse the process. For example, the hexadecimal number 2F63 converts to

$$2 \qquad F \qquad 6 \qquad 3_{16}$$
$$0010 \quad 1111 \quad 0110 \quad 0011_2$$

Note: When you convert 8- or 16-bit binary to hexadecimal, you *do not* supply insignificant 0s. This is because one hexadecimal digit exactly represents half a byte. Sometimes a half byte is called a nibble.

PROCEDURE

Part 1

1. Load the binary-to-hex program.
2. Examine the program to be sure that no errors have been made.
3. Correct any errors.
4. Execute the program.
5. Enter the binary numbers produced by the microprocessor and your hex conversions in a copy of Table 2-7.
6. Ask for the speedup address and increase the speed of the program.

Part 2

1. Load, verify, correct, and execute the hex-to-binary conversion program.
2. Record the hexadecimal numbers and your binary conversions in a copy of Table 2-8.
3. Speed up the program as in preceding steps.

DISCUSSION TOPICS

1. Which notation is easier to use, octal or hexadecimal? Why? Why do you suppose octal notation is popular for use with 12-bit minicom-

Table 2-7 Binary-to-Hexadecimal Conversion

Random Number	Binary	Hex
1		
2		
3		
4		
5		
6		
7		
8		
9		
10		
11		
12		
13		
14		
15		
16		
17		
18		
19		
20		
21		
22		
23		
24		
25		

Table 2-8 Hexadecimal-to-Binary Conversion

Random Number	Hex	Binary
1		
2		
3		
4		
5		
6		
7		
8		
9		
10		
11		
12		
13		
14		
15		
16		
17		
18		
19		
20		
21		
22		
23		
24		
25		

puters and microcomputers? Why did the introduction of 4-, 8-, and 16-bit microprocessors make hexadecimal popular?

2. What kinds of situations will make you convert decimal to hexadecimal (or octal) and hexadecimal (or octal) to decimal?

3. Why do you think some computer languages let the programmer identify the base of a number? For example, you might see 11F2H (hexadecimal), 376–234A (offset octal), 2369D (decimal), and 0110 1101B (binary) all in one program. What does this mean the programmer does not have to do?

4. Why do you suppose other bases were not chosen as shorthand for binary numbers? For example, why are base 10, base 4, and base 32 not used?

CHAPTER | 3

Processor Arithmetic

ACTIVITY 3-1
TEST: PROCESSOR ARITHMETIC

On a separate sheet of paper, complete the following questions.

1. The main difference between the binary and decimal systems is the number of _____ that stand for different quantities.
   a. 1s
   b. 0s
   c. Characters
   d. 9s

2. If you add two digits and the result cannot be expressed as a single digit, you have caused a _____.
   a. Carry
   b. Borrow
   c. Sum
   d. Difference

3. Multiplication is a quick way of doing a lot of _____.
   a. Additions
   b. Subtractions
   c. Divisions
   d. Permutations

4. Each time the multiplicand is multiplied by 1 bit in the multiplier, a _____ is generated.
   a. Sum
   b. Difference
   c. Partial product
   d. Partial quotient

5. An 8-bit 2's complement number represents decimal numbers in the range of _____.
   a. -127 to $+128$
   b. -128 to $+127$
   c. 0 to 255
   d. 0 to 256

6. By multiplying two 8-bit numbers together, it is possible to produce a product as long as _____.
   a. 9 bits   c. 16 bits
   b. 10 bits   d. 2^8 bits

7. Division can be synthesized by _____.
   a. Shifting left
   b. Repeated addition
   c. Repeated multiplication
   d. Repeated subtraction

8. Very large and very small numbers are often represented by using
   _____.
   a. Base 3
   b. BASIC
   c. Floating point
   d. Positional weighting

9. Add the following 8-bit binary numbers and show the status register's contents as well as the 8-bit result. Check your work in decimal.

   a.　　0110 1110　　e.　　1100 1100
   　　+ 0001 0010　　　　+ 1111 0000

   b.　　0010 1100　　f.　　0101 0101
   　　+ 0001 1110　　　　+ 1000 0001

   c.　　1100 0100　　g.　　0011 1100
   　　+ 0011 1000　　　　+ 0101 1010

   d.　　0101 1100　　h.　　1010 1001
   　　+ 0011 1001　　　　+ 0101 0111

10. Subtract the following numbers by using 2's complement arithmetic. If an answer is negative, express it as an unsigned binary number with a minus sign. Show your work. Check your work in decimal.

    a.　　0110 1011　　e.　　0100 1111
    　　− 0001 0100　　　　− 0001 1101

    b.　　0101 1100　　f.　　0111 0000
    　　− 0011 1101　　　　− 0010 1100

    c.　　0011 0011　　g.　　0011 0011
    　　− 0001 0011　　　　− 0100 0001

    d.　　0110 0011　　h.　　0001 1101
    　　− 0010 1100　　　　− 0010 1111

11. Multiply the following 8-bit binary numbers. Express your results as 16-bit binary numbers. Check your results by using decimal arithmetic.

    a.　　0110 1110　　d.　　0101 0101
    　　× 0001 0010　　　　× 0001 0110

    b.　　1011 1100　　e.　　0011 1011
    　　× 0011 0000　　　　× 0010 0000

    c.　　0011 1000　　f.　　1010 1100
    　　× 0000 0110　　　　× 0001 0011

12. Perform the divisions indicated below. Check your work by using decimal arithmetic.

    a. $0011\overline{)1100}$　　c. $0100\overline{)1100}$

    b. $0101\overline{)1111}$　　d. $0010\overline{)1110}$

13. Draw a table of binary division.
14. Draw a table of binary multiplication.

15. Explain why a binary division algorithm for a processor involves a decision.

16. How is a negative number identified in 2's complement arithmetic?

17. In an 8-bit microprocessor, a triple-precision binary number requires one sign bit and how many magnitude bits?

18. In question 17, suppose the number were in floating-point format. Why would a fourth byte be required in that case?

19. Draw a table of binary addition.

20. Draw a table of binary subtraction.

21. What method of floating-point implementation produces the fastest floating-point operation?

ACTIVITY 3-2
LAB EXPERIMENT:
BINARY ADDITION

PURPOSE

In this experiment you will observe the microprocessor carrying out binary addition. You will also gain practice in doing binary addition manually.

MATERIALS

Qty.
1   Microprocessor trainer
1   Program listing

INTRODUCTION

Binary addition is just like decimal addition except that it uses a different addition table. The binary addition table is shown in Fig. 3-1.

Binary addition results in a carry as soon as you add 1 and 1. The carry of 1 must be added to the addend in the next column to the left.

Most microprocessors add either 8- or 16-bit numbers. The full 8 (or 16) bits is used even if the number can be represented by fewer bits. The unused bits to the left of the most significant bit are 0s. These bits are used because the microprocessor must work with its standard word length.

In most cases, we represent binary words by using hexadecimal notation. On rare occasions, octal can be used as well. If you wanted to add, say, 23_{10} and 16_{10}, you would use the following conversions:

$$
\begin{array}{cccc}
23_{10} & 17_{16} & 0001 & 0111_2 \\
+\ 16_{10} & 10_{16} & 0001 & 0000_2 \\
\hline
39_{10} & 27_{16} & 0010 & 0111
\end{array}
$$

In this example, we converted the decimal numbers to hexadecimal. The microprocessor trainer takes the hexadecimal input but actually performs the addition in binary form. To obtain the decimal answer, you must convert the hexadecimal value to decimal.

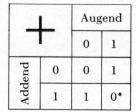

$+$	Augend	
	0	1
Addend 0	0	1
Addend 1	1	0°

°with a carry of 1

Fig. 3-1

PROCEDURE

Part 1

1. Obtain the program listing for the binary addition program from your instructor and enter the program.
2. Verify proper entry of the program.
3. Correct any errors in the program.
4. Obtain the address locations of the addend, augend, and sum. Each location is 1 byte long if you are using an 8-bit machine. Load 3_{16} into the addend memory location.
5. Load 2_{16} into the augend location.
6. Execute the program.
7. Display the contents of the memory location that is reserved for the sum. The result should be 5_{16}, which is also equal to 5_{10}. What is your result?

Part 2

1. The following is a set of addition problems. With pencil and paper, perform the additions manually and then check your answers by using the addition program. Note that decimal and octal numbers will have to be entered in hexadecimal format into most trainers. Also, most trainers will display the sum in hex form.

a. 63_{10}
$+ 29_{10}$

b. 33_{10}
$+ 45_{10}$

c. AF_{16}
$+ 0A_{16}$

d. 263_8
$+ 115_8$

e. 127_{10}
$+ 115_{10}$

f. 251_{10}
$+ 129_{10}$

g. FF_{16}
$+ FF_{16}$

h. 377_8
$+ 137_8$

i. 123_8
$+ 116_8$

j. 221_{10}
$+ 179_{10}$

k. 10_{16}
$+ FA_{16}$

l. 255_{10}
$+ 001_{10}$

Table 3-1

No.	Result			Comments
---	Decimal	Hex	Binary	
a.				
b.				
c.				
d.				
e.				
f.				
g.				
h.				
i.				
j.				
k.				
l.				

2. Copy Table 3-1 and record your answers to the addition problems in question number one. The answers will be entered in decimal, hex, and binary forms.

ACTIVITY 3-3
LAB EXPERIMENT:
BINARY SUBTRACTION

PURPOSE

The purpose of this experiment is to allow you to work with a microprocessor in performing binary subtraction. You will observe that subtraction can be performed by adding the 2's complement of the subtrahend to the minuend.

MATERIALS

Qty.

1 Microprocessor trainer
2 Program listings

INTRODUCTION

Binary subtraction is performed much as normal decimal subtraction is, except that a different subtraction table is used. The binary subtraction table is shown in Fig. 3-2.

Many microprocessors perform subtraction by using 2's complement arithmetic. The 2's complement of a binary number is found by inverting each bit in the number and then adding 1 to the result. For example, to subtract 23_{10} from 56_{10} the following steps would be performed:

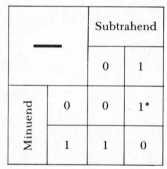

	Subtrahend	
	0	1
Minuend 0	0	1°
Minuend 1	1	0

°with a borrow of 1

Fig. 3-2

1. 23_{10} 0001 0111
2. 1's complement   1110 1000   Making the
3. Add 1   0000 0001   2's complement
4. 2's complement   1110 1001
5. 56   0011 1000
6. 2's complement of 23   1110 1001   Doing the
7. Result 33   1 0010 0001   subtraction

Many microprocessors have a subtract instruction that performs the 2's complement operation automatically. This experiment will investigate both subtraction techniques.

PROCEDURE

Part 1

1. Load the binary addition program that was used in Activity 3-2.
2. Verify correct loading of the program and correct any errors.
3. Load the addend memory location with 56_{10}.
4. Load the augend memory location with the 2's complement of 23_{10}.
5. Execute the program.
6. Display the contents of the memory location that is reserved for the sum. The result should be 33_{10}. Record your result.

Part 2

1. Obtain the binary subtraction program from your instructor and load it into your microprocessor trainer.
2. Verify that loading is correct and, if it is not, correct the errors.
3. Obtain the address locations for the minuend, subtrahend, and difference from your instructor.
4. Load the minuend location with 56_{10}.
5. Load the subtrahend with 23_{10}.
6. Execute the program.
7. Display the contents of the difference memory location. The difference should be 33_{10}. Record your result.

Part 3

1. Manually perform the following subtraction problems and then use the subtraction program to verify your answers. Resolve any differences between your answers and the microprocessor answers. Record your answers on a copy of Table 3-2.

a. 54_{10}
   $- 12_{10}$

b. 48_{10}
   $- 15_{10}$

c. $0F_{16}$
   $- 03_{16}$

d. 17_8
   $- 07_8$

e. 123_8
   $- 117_8$

f. 123_8
   $- 021_8$

g. $7F_{16}$
   $- 3A_{16}$

h. 177_8
   $- 177_8$

i. 29_{10}
   $- 13_{10}$

j. 22_{16}
   $- 6A_{16}$

k. 29_{10}
   $- 39_{10}$

l. 007_8
   $- 177_8$

Table 3-2

| No. | Result | | | Comments |
	Decimal	Hex	Binary	
a.				
b.				
c.				
d.				
e.				
f.				
g.				
h.				
i.				
j.				
k.				
l.				

Note: If the results are negative, place a minus sign in the decimal column. Show the decimal absolute value beside the minus sign.

ACTIVITY 3-4
LAB EXPERIMENT:
BINARY MULTIPLICATION

PURPOSE

This experiment will allow you to check your ability to multiply two binary numbers. You will also observe that the product of two relatively small operands (the multiplier and multiplicand) can easily become quite large.

MATERIALS

Qty.
1 Microprocessor trainer
1 Program listing

INTRODUCTION

Binary multiplication is performed according to the rules illustrated in Fig. 3-3. When a specific multiple-step procedure is used to perform a task, such as multiplication, that procedure is called an *algorithm*.

To perform binary multiplication in a microprocessor, we use an algorithm called *shift and add*. The basis for the shift-and-add algorithm can be seen by looking at a binary multiplication problem. For example, to multiply 15 by 14 we have:

Fig. 3-3

$$
\begin{array}{rr}
1111 & 15 \\
\times 1110 & \times 14 \\
\hline
0000 & 60 \\
1111 & 15 \\
1111 & \\
1111 & \\
\hline
11010010 & 210 \\
\end{array}
$$

You can see that this multiplication is done by multiplying the multiplicand by each bit of the multiplier. As each more significant multiplier bit is used, the partial product is moved over so that its bits have the proper weights. Once all the partial products are developed, they are summed to yield a total product. If the multiplier bit is a 1, then the partial product is identical to the multiplicand. If the multiplier bit is a 0, then the partial product is 0. See the binary multiplication table to check this. In a processor we shift the multiplicand and add. This is done because the shifting and adding are two jobs the processor can do.

PROCEDURE

Part 1

1. Load the binary multiplication program from the listing your teacher gave you.
2. Verify that the program is loaded correctly. If it is not, correct the errors.

3. Your instructor will give you the memory locations that this program uses to store the multiplicand, the multiplier, and the product.
4. Load the multiplicand's memory location with 15_{10}. Remember that you are loading an 8-bit number and so you must load all 8 bits.
5. Load the multiplier's memory location with 14_{10}.
6. Load the product's memory location with 0. *You must do that each time you run this program.* If you do not clear this location (set its contents to 0), you will add the contents to the new product. That is because this program also uses this memory location to store its partial products.
7. Run the program.
8. Display the contents of the product's memory location. It should be 210_{10}. What is your result?

Part 2

1. Use the binary multiplication program to do the following multiplications. Convert each problem to binary and then manually do the binary multiplication. Do that before you use the microprocessor. Use the microprocessor to verify your calculations. Resolve any answers that do not agree. Remember that you must load the multiplicand and the multiplier, *and put a 0 in the product.*

a.	12_{10} $\times\ 4_{10}$	d.	27_8 $\times\ 7_8$	g.	F_{16} $\times\ F_{16}$	j.	5_{16} $\times\ 4_{16}$
b.	9_{10} $\times\ 5_{10}$	e.	101_{10} $\times\ 2_{10}$	h.	17_8 $\times\ 12_8$	k.	28_{10} $\times\ 9_{10}$
c.	F_{16} $\times\ C_{16}$	f.	A_{16} $\times\ B_{16}$	i.	5_{10} $\times\ 4_{10}$	l.	28_{10} $\times\ 10_{10}$

Table 3-3

No.	Result			Comments
	Decimal	Hex	Binary	
a.				
b.				
c.				
d.				
e.				
f.				
g.				
h.				
i.				
j.				
k.				
l.				

2. Complete Table 3-3 on a separate sheet of paper.

DISCUSSION TOPICS

1. How many bits of precision are needed so that you can multiply two four-digit decimal numbers? Relatively speaking, how many bits do you need to do multiplication as compared with addition or subtraction?

2. When you were using the binary arithmetic programs, you had to be sure to enter leading 0s. For example, multiplying 15_{10} by 14_{10} was done by entering $0F_{16}$ and $0E_{16}$ instead of F_{16} and E_{16}. Why do you suppose that is necessary? What would you have had to enter if you had been using an 8-bit microprocessor with triple precision?

CHAPTER | 4

Basic Microprocessor Architectural Concepts

ACTIVITY 4-1
TEST: BASIC MICROPROCESSOR
ARCHITECTURAL CONCEPTS

On a separate sheet of paper, choose the letter that best completes each of the following statements.

1. An example of a 4-bit microprocessor is the _____.
   - *a.* 6800
   - *b.* 8080
   - *c.* 8088
   - *d.* TMS-1000

2. This would not be considered an architectural characteristic of a microprocessor: _____.
   - *a.* Data bus width
   - *b.* Chip manufacturer
   - *c.* Address bus width
   - *d.* The number of registers in the CPU

3. Generally speaking, this results in an increase in processor execution speed: _____.
   - *a.* Increased address bus width
   - *b.* Reduced clock speed
   - *c.* CAD
   - *d.* Increased clock speed

4. Most likely, a 4-bit microprocessor would not be found in _____.
   - *a.* A microwave oven control circuit
   - *b.* A clock
   - *c.* A motor-speed controller
   - *d.* A general-purpose computer

5. The microprocessor used in the IBM PC is the _____.
   - *a.* 8088
   - *b.* TMS-1000
   - *c.* 68HC11
   - *d.* 68000

6. The abbreviation CAD stands for _____.
   a. Computer-aided design
   b. Computer-aided detailing
   c. Computerized axial demonstration
   d. Computer-assisted devices

7. The Digital Equipment Corporation's VAX computer is designed around a(n) _____.
   a. 8-bit microprocessor
   b. 16-bit microprocessor
   c. 32-bit microprocessor
   d. Bit-slice processor

8. Data that must not be allowed to change or be lost is stored in _____.
   a. RAM
   b. ROM
   c. BCD
   d. The microprocessor

9. The program that initializes a microcomputer is called a _____.
   a. Clock program
   b. Boot program
   c. Mass-storage program
   d. Database manager program

10. Compared to CMOS, the NMOS process allows _____.
    a. Operation over a wider voltage range
    b. Operation over a wider temperature range
    c. Operation at higher clock frequencies
    d. All of the above

11. The function of a coprocessor is to _____.
    a. Increase overall system speed
    b. Increase the speed of certain instructions
    c. Add additional instructions to the system
    d. All of the above

12. Data that must be accessed very quickly would be stored in or on _____.
    a. Cache memory
    b. A hard disk
    c. ROM
    d. Dynamic RAM

13. Temporary storage of data within the microprocessor is provided by _____.
    a. Indexes
    b. I/O ports
    c. Registers
    d. Z80

14. Serial I/O is often provided by a device called _____.
    a. A coprocessor
    b. A cross-assembler
    c. An in-circuit emulator
    d. A UART

15. Additional devices that are required for a microprocessor to operate correctly are called _____.
    a. In-circuit emulators
    b. Support chips
    c. UARTs
    d. Assemblers

ACTIVITY 4-2
RESEARCH

PURPOSE

The basic purpose of this activity is to illustrate the wide varieties of microprocessors and architectures available. You will determine the major architectural features of several popular microprocessors.

MATERIALS

General microprocessor information such as computer-related magazines, microprocessor textbooks, electronic parts catalogs, and manufacturers' data sheets or data books.

PROCEDURE

Copy the following table on a separate sheet of paper and supply the information requested. This information can be obtained from the sources listed under "Materials," or you may wish to ask friends or acquaintances who are knowledgeable about microprocessors for help.

	6800 CPU	8088 CPU
Address bus width	_____	_____
Data bus width	_____	_____
Number of 8-bit registers (gen. purpose)	_____	_____
Number of 16-bit registers (gen. purpose)	_____	_____
Number of status bits used	_____	_____
Separate I/O address space? (Y/N)	_____	_____
Instruction queue (cache)? (Y/N)	_____	_____
Optional coprocessor? (Y/N)	_____	_____
Current cost	_____	_____

CHAPTER | 5

Inside the Microprocessor

ACTIVITY 5-1
TEST: INSIDE THE
MICROPROCESSOR

On a separate sheet of paper, complete the following questions.

1. Which of the following is not a major MPU subsection? _____
   a. ALU
   b. Memory
   c. Registers
   d. Control logic

2. To input or output data, a given logic device must have at least one _____.
   a. Register
   b. Bus
   c. Port
   d. Byte

3. The microprocessor's ALU is used to modify data by means of arithmetic or _____.
   a. Subtraction
   b. Logic operations
   c. Concatenation
   d. Addition

4. The main function of a register is to _____.
   a. Modify data
   b. Modify addresses
   c. Shift data
   d. Store data

5. Microprocessors have six fundamental registers. Which of the following is not included in the six? _____
   a. Accumulator
   b. Program counter
   c. General-purpose register
   d. Instruction register

6. During normal program execution, the program counter points to the _____.
   a. Instruction following the one currently being executed
   b. Accumulator
   c. First instruction in memory
   d. Last instruction in memory

7. The ALU outputs data to the _____.
   a. Accumulator
   b. Program counter
   c. General-purpose register
   d. Instruction register

8. If an operation uses the accumulator to add 2 bytes together, one of the bytes will usually be located in the _____.
   a. Accumulator
   b. Program counter
   c. Index register
   d. Instruction register

9. The microprocessor's most versatile register is the _____.
   a. Accumulator
   b. Program counter
   c. Condition-code register
   d. Instruction register

10. Assuming a given microprocessor has an 8-bit data bus, the accumulator of such a microprocessor will most likely be _____ bits wide.
   a. 4   *c.* 16
   b. 8   *d.* 32

11. A microprocessor with an address range of 65,536 words has a program counter that is _____ bits wide.
   a. 4
   b. 8
   c. 16
   d. 32

12. A certain microprocessor has a 20-bit address bus. Approximately how many words of memory can be addressed by this microprocessor? _____
   a. 64K
   b. 256K
   c. 1M
   d. 10M

13. The program counter _____.
   a. Keeps track of the data bus
   b. Keeps track of carry-outs of the MSB
   c. Keeps track of which instruction is executed next
   d. Does none of the above

14. When a microprocessor initially starts up, the first instruction address is _____.
   a. Located at the beginning of memory
   b. Located at the end of memory
   c. Always the same
   d. Found in the accumulator

15. The program counter points to a memory location, and the control logic _____ the instruction.
   a. Executes   *c.* Stores
   b. Fetches   *d.* Clears

16. Once the instruction is in the instruction register, the program counter points to the _____ instruction.
  a. Fetched
  b. Next
  c. Control
  d. Program

17. Once the program counter is pointed to a certain area in memory, it increments from one instruction to _____.
  a. The next *sequential instruction*
  b. The next data byte
  c. The next data word
  d. All of the above

18. Executing an arithmetic or logic instruction may set certain bits in what register? _____
  a. The instruction register
  b. The general-purpose register
  c. The status register
  d. The memory address register

19. Often the program's direction is changed by the results of testing a bit in the _____ register.
  a. Instruction
  b. General-purpose
  c. Status
  d. Memory address

20. When an instruction is fetched, it is copied into the _____ register.
  a. Status
  b. Instruction
  c. Memory address
  d. General-purpose

21. The microprocessor's _____ determines what an instruction is to do and makes the microprocessor execute it.
  a. ALU
  b. MPU
  c. Control logic
  d. Instruction register

22. An instruction is a unique _____ indicating that a specific operation is to be done.
  a. Binary word
  b. Address
  c. Logic function
  d. Destination

23. The control logic uses a timing signal called _____ to ensure that operations are carried out in the proper sequence.
  a. An oscillator
  b. A TTL drive
  c. A clock
  d. A crystal

24. The microprocessor's logic functions communicate with one another by the _____.
  a. Address bus   *c.* Communicator bus
  b. Internal data bus *d.* Arithmetic logic unit

25. When one logic function sends data to another, the sender is termed the "source" and the receiver is termed the _____.
  a. Destination   *c.* ALU
  b. Operand   *d.* Variable

26. Briefly explain the function of the microprocessor's memory address register.

27. How wide would you expect the memory address register to be in a microprocessor with 4M memory words?

28. A certain register may be considered to consist of a high word and a low word. The register is part of a 16-bit microprocessor. How wide would you expect this register to be? Why?

29. List the six registers common to all microprocessors.

30. Write a brief description of the function of each of the six registers found in any microprocessor.

31. What result did an arithmetic instruction cause if the carry bit was set after the instruction was executed?

32. What result did an arithmetic instruction cause if you find that the zero bit was cleared after the instruction was executed?

33. What result did an arithmetic instruction cause if the negative bit was set after the instruction was executed?

ACTIVITY 5-2
LAB EXPERIMENT:
EXAMINING THE
MICROPROCESSOR'S REGISTERS

PURPOSE

This experiment has two objectives. First, you will become more familiar with the registers in your specific microprocessor. Second, you will become more familiar with the microprocessor trainer keyboard functions, specifically, the functions that allow observation and manipulation of register contents.

MATERIALS

Qty.
1   Microprocessor trainer
1   Instruction/operator's manual for microprocessor trainer

INTRODUCTION

In preceding experiments you used the microprocessor trainer keyboard to enter programs and data into memory. In addition, you also corrected and changed (edited) program instructions and data in various programs. All these are important keyboard functions.

Your microprocessor trainer will also allow you to examine and in most cases modify the contents of the microprocessor's working registers. For example, you can load and verify the contents of the accumulator. You can also load and verify the contents of the program counter.

Of course, the microprocessor's registers are actually inside the integrated circuit. The only connections between the registers and the outside world are the internal and external data buses. There is no true direct connection between the keyboard or the display and the register you wish to examine.

The microprocessor trainer allows registers to be examined and modified through the use of a program stored in ROM. This program, called the monitor program, contains a shorter section of code (instructions) that reads the keyboard and carries out the operation indicated by the key that is pressed. Say, for example, that you press the key that allows examination of the accumulator. The monitor program will copy the contents of the accumulator into the display or into a memory location where the display looks for data to display.

PROCEDURE

1. Power up your microprocessor trainer and display the contents of the accumulator. Note: The exact keys you must press to do so depend on your particular trainer. Some trainers have a single key to examine each register; others may use a single key to activate a Display Register mode. In the latter case, a second key or set of keys displays the desired register.
2. Copy Table 5-1. Fill in the Original Contents column of your copy with the contents of each register listed as you find them. Make note of whether the data is displayed in binary, hex, octal, or decimal form in the Data Format column. If your processor has more than one accumulator, use accumulator A or its equivalent.
3. Once you have completed Step 2, return to displaying the contents of the accumulator.
4. Starting with the accumulator, modify the contents of each register by loading new data. Most microprocessor trainers require the current contents of a given register to be displayed before they can be changed. Generally, to change register contents, a *change* or *modify* key must be pressed, followed by the hex or possibly the binary data.
5. Choose new data for each register as you see fit. Record the data you entered in the Data Loaded column of your copy of Table 5-1. If the contents of a particular register cannot be modified, make a note of the occurrence in the Comments column.
6. After all registers have been modified, reexamine the register contents and record the displayed contents in the New Contents column. Again, if the contents of a given register prove to be unaltered, make note of the fact in the Comments column.
7. If possible, attempt to enter an illegal number into a register. For example, try to enter a third hex digit into an 8-bit register.
8. Experiment with the trainer until you are comfortable with the procedure used to display and modify register contents.

DISCUSSION TOPICS

1. Is it possible to access all six of the fundamental microprocessor registers? If not, list the registers that cannot be accessed.

Table 5-1

Register	Original Contents	Data Format	Data Loaded	New Contents	Comments
Accumulator					
Program counter					
Register pair					
Status register					
Index register					

CHAPTER | 6

An Introduction to Microprocessor Instructions

ACTIVITY 6-1
TEST: AN INTRODUCTION
TO MICROPROCESSOR
INSTRUCTIONS

On a separate sheet of paper, choose the letter that best applies to the following statements and questions.

1. Most microprocessor instructions are designed to _____.
    a. Move data
    b. Process data
    c. Clear registers
    d. Move or process data

2. A complete list of all the microprocessor's instructions is called
    _____.
    a. Op code
    b. Read-only memory
    c. Mnemonics
    d. The instruction set

3. An instruction is made up of an address or operand and the
    _____.
    a. Op code
    b. Assembler
    c. Mnemonic
    d. Condition code

4. Short abbreviations that represent instructions are called _____.
    a. Op codes
    b. Mnemonics
    c. Operands
    d. Addresses

5. Usually, the second and third words in an instruction are used for
    data or to represent _____.
    a. Addresses
    b. Op codes
    c. Mnemonics
    d. Instruction sets

6. An instruction that consists of an op code followed by a data word uses this addressing mode: _____.
   a. Direct
   b. Inherent or implied
   c. Immediate
   d. Indirect

7. An instruction that does not require explicit identification of the data or its address uses this addressing mode: _____.
   a. Direct
   b. Inherent or implied
   c. Immediate
   d. Indirect

8. An instruction the second word of which points to the address of the data to be manipulated uses this mode of addressing: _____.
   a. Direct
   b. Inherent or implied
   c. Immediate
   d. Indirect

9. The data that a given instruction manipulates is referred to as an _____.
   a. Operand
   b. Operator
   c. Operation
   d. Op code

10. A shortened form of addressing is often used on 8-bit microprocessors that have a 64K addressing range. These instructions have only one address byte. Normally, this limits the range of access of these instructions to page 0. Page 0 is the first _____.
    a. Byte of ROM
    b. I/O port
    c. 32 bytes of memory
    d. 256 bytes of memory

11. The relative speed of execution of a given instruction is found by counting the number of _____ it uses.
    a. Seconds
    b. MPU cycles
    c. Bits
    d. Bytes

12. This register is often used for addressing data in a sequential list: _____.
    a. Accumulator
    b. Stack pointer
    c. HL register
    d. Index register

13. A byte used to represent a relative address would be interpreted to be this type of number: _____.
    a. 1's complement
    b. 2's complement
    c. Positive
    d. Negative

14. This addressing mode requires fewer memory locations per instruction than direct addressing: _____.
    a. Indexed addressing   c. Relative addressing
    b. Extended addressing   d. Inherent addressing

15. A relative address that lies at a lower address than the current contents of the program counter would be indicated by _____.
   a. The setting of the N flag to logic 1
   b. A single-word instruction
   c. A 1 in the MSB of the relative address
   d. A 0 in the MSB of the relative address

16. Subroutines are entered via execution of the _____ instruction.
   a. CALL
   b. RET
   c. IRET
   d. IN

17. The operation "Load register r with the contents of the location pointed to by the HL register pair" is represented mnemonically by _____.
   a. LD r,(HL)
   b. LD (HL),r
   c. LD r,n
   d. LD r,HL

18. The hex numbers AA_{16} and $9F_{16}$ are logically ANDed together. The resulting hex number is _____.
   a. BF_{16}
   b. AA_{16}
   c. $9A_{16}$
   d. $8A_{16}$

19. A certain 8-bit register contains the packed BCD quantity 1001 0101. If we attempt to unpack this quantity by shifting right four times, the register will contain the decimal value _____ after the operation.
   a. 95
   b. 05
   c. 90
   d. 09

20. When a subroutine is called from within another subroutine, we are said to have _____.
   a. An interrupt
   b. A nested subroutine
   c. A recursion
   d. A stack overflow

21. The job of an assembler is to convert _____ into _____.
   a. Numbers, mnemonics
   b. Source code, object code
   c. Addresses, data
   d. Data, addresses

Briefly answer the following questions.

22. Explain how a microprocessor's instruction set can have the same op code used in a number of different instructions.

23. We say that the object of an op code is the op code's operand. What does that mean?

24. You are using a 16-bit microprocessor that has a 64K address range, and you find that each of the instructions is either one or two words long. Explain how the microprocessor can have inherent, immediate, direct, and indirect addressing if it has only two words when a similar 8-bit microprocessor takes three words.

25. Briefly explain how indirect addressing is different from inherent addressing.

26. Indirect addressing is faster than direct addressing only when you need to address the same memory locations a number of times. Why?

ACTIVITY 6-2
RESEARCH:
SURVEYING YOUR
MICROPROCESSOR'S
ADDRESSING MODES

PURPOSE

The text has presented you with a simplified but representative microprocessor that offers four addressing modes. In this activity, you will study the actual addressing modes that are used by your microprocessor.

MATERIALS

Qty.
1   Microprocessor trainer instruction manual

INTRODUCTION

These addressing modes allow you to locate data in four distinct ways. All microprocessors have different addressing modes available. In fact, all commercially available microprocessors have at least inherent, direct, and immediate addressing modes.

Recall that inherent addressing is also called implied addressing. An instruction that uses inherent addressing is one word long. Such an instruction implies that the operand is located within some specific register in the microprocessor.

Immediate addressing dictates that the operand referred to by the op code be located in the memory location immediately following the op code itself. Generally, immediate addressing is used to load constant data into registers. That is, immediate operands are usually numerical values that will not be altered when the program is executed.

When the instruction op code is followed immediately by the address of the operand, direct addressing is being used. That is, the word or words following the op code "directs" the microprocessor to the location of the data. This addressing mode is useful when data is located in a section of memory other than where the program itself is located.

Indexed addressing is often used when long lists of data must be accessed sequentially. Items in the list can be processed one at a time in succession by incrementing the index register and, of course, using indexed addressing.

Relative addressing is used most often when execution of a program is to continue out of the normal path of instructions. Two's complement values are normally used in this addressing mode. Thus, forward and backward branching may occur. Relative addressing is also necessary for the creation of relocatable code.

Many other possible addressing modes are in use with different microprocessors. An example is register-indirect addressing. In this addressing mode, a single-word instruction indicates a specific register whose contents are the address of the operand. Other and more complex variations of this mode also are used.

PROCEDURE

1. Review the instruction manual for your microprocessor trainer and list the different addressing modes available. A data book containing information on the microprocessor you are using may also be used to find this information. Write a brief description of each addressing mode.

2. Determine which addressing modes on your machine are equivalent to inherent, immediate, and direct addressing modes as described in the text. Be careful not to confuse page 0 direct addressing with "extended" or "full" direct addressing.

   Inherent addressing _____

   Immediate addressing _____

   Direct addressing _____

3. There may be addressing modes that do not address memory locations but instead address input/output (I/O) locations. If such addressing modes are available, list them.

DISCUSSION TOPICS

Investigate the addressing modes available for other microprocessors. This requires consultation with various processor data books and data sheets. Some microprocessors, such as the 8088, have relatively complex addressing modes in addition to the basic modes presented so far.

ACTIVITY 6-3
LAB EXPERIMENT:
LOADING, MOVING, AND STORING DATA

PURPOSE

The movement of data from memory to register, register to memory, register to register, and memory to memory are some of the most fundamental operations that a microprocessor must perform. This experiment demonstrates the operation of your microprocessor's load, store, and move instructions.

NOTE

Since microprocessor instruction sets are in general rather complex, not all groups of instructions will be introduced and demonstrated under the heading of Chap. 6. The reason for the limitation is simply to keep you from being overwhelmed by the subject. So, as you progress from this point, the different groups of instructions will be introduced in activities for successive chapters in addition to chapter-specific activities.

MATERIALS

Qty.

1 Microprocessor trainer
1 Instruction set listing

INTRODUCTION

The load instructions are used to copy data from a memory location to a register. They are usually used near the beginning of a program to preset registers to known values. Load instructions are also used to transfer data from memory to registers during the working part of a program.

Generally speaking, the store instructions are used to copy the contents of a register into a memory location; thus, they are complementary to load instructions. Often when a specific register must be used for several purposes, the contents of the register are stored temporarily in memory while the register is used in some other manner. The original contents of the register are then restored by using a load instruction.

Move instructions are normally used to copy the contents of one register into another, but can also often be used to perform the same operations as load and store instructions. Move instructions can also be used to transfer data directly from one memory location to another. Thus, move instructions are more generalized in their applications than load and store instructions are. The penalty paid for this flexibility is longer execution time and often more memory usage per instruction.

The availability of different addressing modes makes the data transfer instructions much more useful. The immediate mode is often used to load constants into registers. Move instructions usually use the inherent mode, especially for register-to-register transfers. Both load and store instructions use direct and indirect addressing modes. Direct addressing is used when data is to be copied into or from a single specific memory location. Indirect addressing is normally used when data is copied into or from varying or sequential memory locations.

PROCEDURE

Part 1

1. Draw the flowchart for a program that will copy the contents of memory location 60_{16} into location 50_{16}.
2. Write a program listing for the flowchart by using your microprocessor's instructions. Use direct addressing where possible.
3. Load the program into the trainer. Manually clear location 50_{16} and enter AA_{16} into location 60_{16}.
4. Single-step through the program to be sure that the program works. Remember, your program will probably be entered starting at address 0000_{16}, so the program counter must be set to that value before single-stepping through the program.
5. Execute the program in the normal mode. Do you obtain the same results?

Part 2

1. Let us enhance the preceding program. Draw the flowchart for a program that will swap the contents of locations 50_{16} and 60_{16}. Use the microprocessor's B register (accumulator B, for example) for any temporary storage that might be needed.
2. Write the machine-language program for your flowchart. Use direct addressing where possible.
3. Load the program and enter AA_{16} into location 50_{16} and BB_{16} into location 60_{16}.
4. Single-step through the program to be sure that the program works properly. Monitor the program counter on this pass.
5. If the program works correctly, single-step through it again, monitoring the accumulator (B), the program counter, and the two memory locations being swapped.
6. Run the program several times. Note that the contents of the memory

locations are swapped back and forth on consecutive runs of the program.

Part 3

1. The swap program will now be enhanced even further. Draw the flowchart for a program that will swap the contents of memory locations 50_{16} and 60_{16} and retain the original contents of the B register (again, accumulator B, or equivalent). To accomplish this, you must save the B register contents temporarily in memory. If your program begins at address 0000_{16}, you would probably be safe in designating address 30_{16} for temporary storage.
2. Code the program and enter it into your trainer.
3. Single-step through the program to make sure that the program works.
4. Execute the program normally several times and verify data swapping. Try using different data in locations 50_{16} and 60_{16}, and retest the program.

DISCUSSION TOPICS

Given a specific microprocessor and a specific job to perform, one can often write a specific program that is much shorter than a generalized program that is capable of doing the same job plus others. For example, the program written in Part 3 was more generalized than that in Part 1. State some possible advantages and disadvantages of generalized and very task-specific programs.

CHAPTER | 7

Communicating with the Microprocessor

ACTIVITY 7-1
TEST: COMMUNICATING
WITH THE MICROPROCESSOR

On a separate sheet of paper, complete the following statements and questions.

1. Microcomputers communicate with the outside world via _____.
   a. Registers
   b. Ports
   c. Control buses
   d. Address buses

2. Ports that are assigned addresses within the same space as the RAM and ROM are said to be _____.
   a. I/O ports
   b. Input ports
   c. Output ports
   d. Memory-mapped

3. Memory locations are not usually _____.
   a. Single-ported
   b. Dual-ported
   c. Memory-mapped
   d. RAM or ROM

4. Generally, data transferred from the outside world into a computer via an I/O port _____.
   a. Is transferred directly to memory
   b. Is transferred directly to the ALU
   c. Is transferred directly to the program counter
   d. Is transferred directly to a register

5. This type of I/O allows an external device to stop the current activity of the microprocessor and request service: _____.
   a. Polled I/O
   b. Interrupt-driven I/O
   c. Programmed I/O
   d. Serial I/O

6. In a system with memory-mapped I/O, the I/O ports receive control signals from _____.

    a. The same control bus as memory devices

    b. A separate I/O control bus

    c. An external device such as a printer

    d. The ALU

7. The Z80 microprocessor effectively has an I/O address bus that is 8 bits wide. Thus, the Z80 may address up to _____ I/O ports.

    a. 8

    b. 255

    c. 256

    d. 64K

8. An interrupt input is similar to _____.

    a. A polling routine

    b. An I/O service routine

    c. A vector

    d. A hardware subroutine call

9. The starting address of an interrupt service routine is contained in _____.

    a. An I/O port

    b. An interrupt vector

    c. A polling routine

    d. An interrupt request input

10. The last instruction in any interrupt service routine is _____.

    a. A return instruction

    b. A halt instruction

    c. A software-interrupt instruction

    d. An interrupt vector

11. This interrupt has the highest priority: _____.

    a. Reset

    b. Nonmaskable interrupt

    c. Maskable interrupt

    d. Software interrupt

12. Masking the interrupts would cause this interrupt to be ignored: _____.

    a. Reset

    b. Nonmaskable interrupt

    c. Maskable interrupt

    d. Power off

13. This type of I/O generally results in the fastest transfer of data between the computer and the I/O device: _____.

    a. Polled I/O

    b. Programmed I/O

    c. Memory-mapped I/O

    d. Direct memory access

14. When an interrupt occurs, the microprocessor should never _____.

    a. Branch to an interrupt service routine

    b. Load an address vector into the program counter

    c. Ignore the interrupt request

    d. Honor the interrupt before completion of the current instruction

15. Describe the difference between an I/O-mapped port and a memory-mapped port.

16. Explain why prioritized interrupts are sometimes used in microprocessor-based systems.

17. Describe the difference between maskable and nonmaskable interrupts. Which type would be considered to have higher priority?

ACTIVITY 7-2
LAB EXPERIMENT:
ARITHMETIC OPERATIONS

PURPOSE

This experiment will familiarize you with the uses of the add, add-with-carry, and subtract instructions. The uses of various addressing modes will be investigated, and the implementation of triple-precision addition will also be presented.

MATERIALS

Qty.

1 Microprocessor trainer
1 Microprocessor instruction set listing

INTRODUCTION

Input/output operations are used to allow the computer to take data from and send data to the outside world. While data is inside the computer, it is often processed by using various arithmetic instructions. All microprocessor instruction sets include the add instruction. Some microprocessors also include instructions that allow direct multiplication and division, although those operations can easily be implemented by using repeated addition and repeated subtraction, respectively.

PROCEDURE

Part 1

1. The flowchart in Fig. 7-1 represents the addition of two 8-bit numbers. The numbers are to be addend = 75_{16} and augend = $4A_{16}$. By using immediate addressing and the add instruction, write the program that will accomplish this task. Don't forget to end your program with a halt instruction or its equivalent. In general, your program should look like the one shown below, which is written in 6802 code. All numerical values are in hex.

Address	Mnemonic	Op Code/Data	Comment
0000	LDAA	86	Immediate mode
0001	75	75	Addend
0002	ADDA	3B	Add immediate to accum. A
0003	4A	4A	Augend
0004	WAI	3E	HALT

2. Load your program and verify correct entry.
3. Single-step through the program and verify correct operation. Record the hex value of the sum. This will, of course, be found in the accumulator.
   Sum = _____
4. Examine the carry flag and record its state. It should be clear.
   C = _____
5. Change the augend to $C0_{16}$ and execute the program. Record the resulting sum and the state of the carry flag after the run. Explain your findings.
   Sum = _____   C = _____

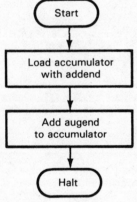

Fig. 7-1

42

6. Modify the program so that three numbers are added.
7. Execute the new program by using three operands of your choice and verify correct operation.
8. Write the code for the flowchart of Fig. 7-1 by using direct addressing. Reserve address locations 30_{16} and 31_{16} for the operands (the addend and the augend).
9. Your program should be similar to the 6802 program listing below.

Address	Mnemonic	Op Code/Data	Comment
0000	LDAA	96	Load ACCA direct
0001	30	30	Address of addend
0002	ADDA	9B	Add to ACCA direct
0003	31	31	Address of augend
0004	HLT	3E	The end

10. Enter and execute your program. Experiment with different values of the operands.
11. Replace the add direct instruction with the direct-mode instruction subtract from accumulator A. In 6802 machine code, this instruction has the mnemonic SUBA and the hex op code is 90_{16}.
12. As the program is currently written, address location 30_{16} contains the minuend and location 31_{16} contains the subtrahend. Execute the program by using the operand values listed below. Record the states of the Z (zero) and N (negative) flags after each run.

Minuend	Subtrahend	Difference	Z	N
$F0_{16}$	$A5_{16}$	_____	_____	_____
$1A_{16}$	10_{16}	_____	_____	_____
$B2_{16}$	$B0_{16}$	_____	_____	_____
35_{16}	09_{16}	_____	_____	_____
AA_{16}	AA_{16}	_____	_____	_____
02_{16}	03_{16}	_____	_____	_____
00_{16}	FF_{16}	_____	_____	_____

13. Perform the subtraction problems manually. Explain any discrepancies between your answers and the microprocessor answers.

Part 2

1. Recall that multiple-precision arithmetic was described in Chap. 3 of the text. Multiple precision allows the microprocessor to perform arithmetic on larger numbers than it normally could. The flowchart in Fig. 7-2 shows the general procedure for adding two 24-bit (triple-precision) numbers. Note that the addition is performed 1 byte at a time as in normal addition except that, when a carry out of the MSB of a given byte occurs, that carry is added to the LSBs of the next more significant byte. For an example of the process, see Fig. 7-3.

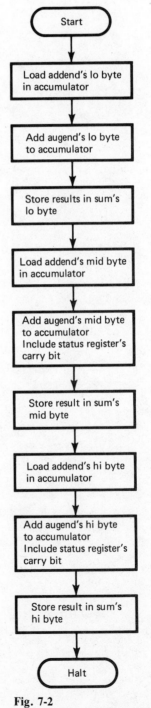

Fig. 7-2

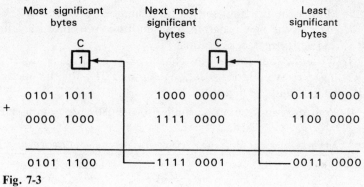

Most significant bytes   Next most significant bytes   Least significant bytes

	Most significant bytes	Next most significant bytes	Least significant bytes
+	0101 1011	1000 0000	0111 0000
	0000 1000	1111 0000	1100 0000
	0101 1100	1111 0001	0011 0000

Fig. 7-3

2. Write a program that will perform the triple-precision addition flow-chart. Use direct addressing and assign addend, augend, and sum storage locations as follows:

Hex Address	Reserved for
0040	Least significant byte of addend
0041	Next most significant byte of addend
0042	Most significant byte of addend
0043	Least significant byte of augend
0044	Next most significant byte of augend
0045	Most significant byte of augend
0046	Least significant byte of sum
0047	Next most significant byte of sum
0048	Most significant byte of sum

3. Your program should look similar to the one listed below. Again, this program is written in 6802 machine code.

Address	Mnemonic	Op Code/Data	Comment
0000	LDAA	96	Load ACCA direct
0001	40	40	Address of LSB of addend
0002	ADDA	9B	Add direct to ACCA
0003	43	43	Address of LSB of augend
0004	STAA	97	Store ACCA direct
0005	46	46	Address of LSB of sum
0006	LDAA	96	Load ACCA direct
0007	41	41	Address of mid-byte of addend
0008	ADCA	99	Add with carry to ACCA direct
0009	44	44	Address of mid-byte of augend
000A	STAA	97	Store ACCA direct
000B	47	47	Address of mid-byte of sum
000C	LDAA	96	Load ACCA direct
000D	42	42	Address of MSB of addend
000E	ADCA	99	Add with carry to ACCA direct
000F	45	45	Address of MSB of augend
0010	STAA	97	Store ACCA direct
0011	48	48	Address of MSB of sum
0012	WAI	3E	The end

44

4. A more compact listing of the program is shown below. The presence of brackets around a number such as [40] indicates that the number is the address of an operand. Immediate operands (not used here) are not enclosed in brackets.

0000	96	40	LDAA [40]
0002	9B	43	ADDA [43]
0004	97	46	STAA [46]
0006	96	41	LDAA [41]
0008	99	44	ADCA [44]
000A	97	47	STAA [47]
000C	96	42	LDAA [42]
000E	99	45	ADCA [45]
0010	97	47	STAA [47]
0012	3E		WAI

5. Load the program and use it to solve the following decimal addition problems.

a. 10   b. 100   c. 65,256   1,500,000
  + 10   + 50   + 8,124   + 262,144

6. Test the limits of the program by adding different numbers.

CHAPTER | 8

Two 8-bit Microprocessors: The Z80 and 6802

ACTIVITY 8-1
TEST: TWO 8-BIT
MICROPROCESSORS:
THE Z80 AND 6802

On a separate sheet of paper, choose the letter that best completes the following statements and questions.

1. The Zilog Z80 could be described as a(n) _____ microprocessor.
   a. ASCII
   b. Obsolete
   c. Unpopular
   d. 8-bit

2. If a character is represented in ASCII code and an eighth bit is used, that bit is used for _____.
   a. Error checking
   b. Error correction
   c. BCD digits
   d. Nothing

3. The architecture of the Z80 is based on that of the _____ microprocessor.
   a. 6502
   b. 6802
   c. 8080
   d. 8088

4. The inclusion of an alternate register set enables the Z80 to easily handle _____.
   a. Multiple-precision arithmetic
   b. Switching from execution of one program to another
   c. ASCII code words
   d. I/O operations

5. When the Z80 is reset, the program counter is initialized to _____.
   a. Address zero
   b. The start of ROM
   c. The same value as the stack pointer
   d. The same value as the IX register

6. The Z80 maskable interrupt has _____ modes of operation.
   a. Two
   b. Three
   c. Four
   d. A user-defined number of

7. The Z80 acronym RST stands for _____.
   a. Reset
   b. Restart
   c. Rest
   d. Resident software timer

8. There are eight RST instructions. The binary identification of each is provided by the external device on address lines _____.
   a. A_0 through A_2
   b. A_3 through A_5
   c. A_5 through A_8
   d. A_7 through A_{15}

9. This type of Z80 maskable interrupt mode does not require the external device to provide an interrupt vector: _____.
   a. Mode 0
   b. Mode 1
   c. Mode 2
   d. Modes 0 and 1

10. When an interrupt is initiated, the contents of the program counter are saved in this location: _____.
    a. The IX register
    b. The accumulator
    c. The interrupt vector
    d. The stack

11. Program counter contents are changed in a nonsequential manner by _____.
    a. PUSH and POP instructions
    b. Register exchange instructions
    c. 8-bit load instructions
    d. Jump and call instructions

12. Execution of a call instruction causes the current contents of the program counter to be _____.
    a. Popped from the stack
    b. Pushed onto the stack
    c. Overwritten and lost
    d. None of the above

13. Z80 I/O devices occupy space in the _____.
    a. I/O address space
    b. Memory address space
    c. Alternate register set
    d. None of the above

14. A slow memory or an I/O device could signal the Z80 that it is not ready for data transfer by _____.
    a. Driving $\overline{BUSREQ}$ low
    b. Driving $\overline{BUSREQ}$ high
    c. Driving $\overline{WAIT}$ low
    d. Driving $\overline{WAIT}$ high

15. Before the Z80 PIO can be used, it must first be _____ or sent configuration instructions.
    a. Initialized   c. Daisy-chained
    b. Tristated   d. None of the above

16. These are classified as Z80 system control lines: _____.
    a. D_0 through D_7
    b. A_0 through A_{15}
    c. $\overline{MI}$, $\overline{MREQ}$, $\overline{IORQ}$, $\overline{RD}$, $\overline{WR}$, and $\overline{RFSH}$
    d. $\overline{HALT}$, $\overline{NMI}$, $\overline{INT}$, $\overline{BUSACK}$, $\overline{BUSREQ}$, $\overline{RESET}$, and $\overline{WAIT}$

17. Relative to the Z80, the Motorola 6802 is considered to be a _____ microprocessor.
    a. Register-intensive
    b. Memory-intensive
    c. Rudely insensitive
    d. First-generation

18. The 6802's reset vector is located _____.
    a. At the beginning of memory
    b. Near the end of memory
    c. In the interrupt vector register
    d. In the reset vector register

19. Any time that an interrupt is processed by the 6802, the contents of all registers except the _____ are saved in the stack.
    a. Stack pointer
    b. Program counter
    c. Index register
    d. Condition code register

20. The 6802's branch instructions use _____.
    a. Direct addressing
    b. Indexed addressing
    c. Extended addressing
    d. Relative addressing

21. The 6802 contains 128 bytes of internal RAM. The first 32 bytes may be powered by a battery. This effectively produces a small section of RAM that retains data after power is turned off. Such RAM is called _____.
    a. Static RAM
    b. Dynamic RAM
    c. Read-only RAM
    d. Nonvolatile RAM

22. The 6802's enable, $R/\overline{W}$, and $\overline{VMA}$ lines make up the _____.
    a. CPU control lines
    b. System control lines
    c. I/O control lines
    d. Handshaking lines

23. The function of the 6802's $\overline{VMA}$ line is to _____.
    a. Signal to external devices the presence of a valid memory address
    b. Allow external devices to take over the address bus
    c. Activate input and output ports
    d. Control handshaking lines on the 6821 PIA

24. The 6802's XTAL and EXTAL lines provide _____.
    a. Maskable and nonmaskable interrupt inputs
    b. Handshaking between the 6802 and the 6821 PIA
    c. Connections between an internal oscillator and a crystal
    d. None of the above.

25. An external device such as a memory device may slow down the 6802 by asserting the _____.
    a. Memory-ready input   c. $\overline{RESET}$ line
    b. Bus-available line   d. $\overline{IRQ}$ line

26. The 6802 does not have the capability to _____.
  a. Tristate the data bus
  b. Mask interrupts
  c. Tristate the address bus
  d. Do any of the above

ACTIVITY 8-2
LAB EXPERIMENT:
BCD ARITHMETIC

PURPOSE

This experiment will introduce you to several new instructions, and it will acquaint you with BCD arithmetic as it is performed by a microprocessor. In addition, the concepts of packing and unpacking BCD data, as well as masking, will be investigated.

MATERIALS

Qty.
1   Microprocessor trainer
1   Instruction set listing

INTRODUCTION

Both the Z80 and the 6802 have provisions for performing arithmetic operations on binary-coded decimal (BCD) numbers. Recall that a BCD digit is a 4-bit quantity that may represent any of the decimal digits (0 through 9). Thus, only 10 of the possible 16 patterns of 1s and 0s are used per BCD digit. The normal binary bit patterns for values greater than 9 are invalid. The advantage of BCD is that it is easy for humans to convert from BCD into decimal and vice versa. In addition, BCD is commonly generated at the outputs of digital circuits that are designed to be interfaced to seven-segment numeric displays such as calculators and clocks.

Because BCD numbers have six invalid or illegal states, it is possible that normal binary addition of two BCD numbers will produce an invalid result. That is shown in Fig. 8-1, where the LSD of the answer is invalid. To obtain the correct result, 6_{10} (0110_2) is added to the LSD. In fact, any time an illegal BCD digit is produced, 6 must be added to that digit to correct the result. That also is shown in Fig. 8-1. If a carry is made from the lower nibble to the higher nibble, 6_{10} must be added to the result to produce the correct sum. That is shown in Fig. 8-2. Such a carry is called a half-carry or auxiliary carry, and the 6802 and Z80 microprocessors have flags that are set when half-carries occur. Finally, if an addition results in illegal BCD values in both positions, 66_{10} is added to the result to obtain the correct answer. Most microprocessors have instructions that automatically perform these corrections.

The preceding examples used what is called packed BCD, that is, two BCD digits packed into each byte. Packing is done to reduce the amount of memory that is used by the BCD data.

```
    0011 0101   BCD ──→   35
+                               +
    0010 0111   BCD ──→   27
    ─────────                ──
    0101 1100   BCD ──→   5?
+         0110   ADD       6
    ─────────
    0110 0010   BCD ──→   62
```

Fig. 8-1

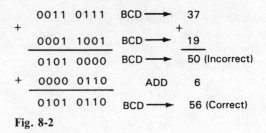

	0011 0111	BCD	→	37	
+				+	
	0001 1001	BCD	→	19	
	0101 0000	BCD	→	50	(Incorrect)
+	0000 0110	ADD		6	
	0101 0110	BCD	→	56	(Correct)

Fig. 8-2

PROCEDURE

Part 1

1. The flowchart in Fig. 8-3 shows how two 2-digit unpacked BCD numbers can be packed. The addresses of the numbers are assigned as follows:

   0030 LSD of unpacked BCD number

   0031 MSD of unpacked BCD number

   0032 packed BCD number

   We assume that the most significant nibbles of the unpacked BCD digits are zero. A 6802 program that will implement this flowchart using these addresses is as follows.

0000	96 30	LDAA [30]	Load ACCA with LSD
0002	D6 31	LDAB [31]	Load ACCB with MSD
0004	58	ASLB	
0005	58	ASLB	Shift MSD over into high nibble
0006	58	ASLB	
0007	58	ASLB	
0008	1B	ABA	Add ACCB to ACCA
0009	3E	WAI	The end

   After execution of this program, accumulator A will contain the packed BCD number.

2. Enter and execute the above program by using a few different unpacked BCD values in address locations 30_{16} and 31_{16}.

3. By using the above packing routine, write a program that will add together two 2-digit BCD numbers. The numbers are initially unpacked and stored as defined below.

   0030 LSD of unpacked BCD augend

   0031 MSD of unpacked BCD augend

   0032 LSD of unpacked BCD addend

   0033 MSD of unpacked BCD addend

   Any temporary storage required should begin at address 0034.

4. The following is a program listing that performs the packing and addition of two 2-digit BCD numbers.

0000	96 30	LDAA [30]	Pack augend
0002	D6 31	LDAB [31]	
0004	58	ASLB	
0005	58	ASLB	

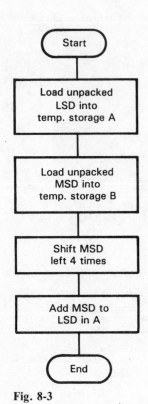

Fig. 8-3

(Flowchart boxes: Start → Load unpacked LSD into temp. storage A → Load unpacked MSD into temp. storage B → Shift MSD left 4 times → Add MSD to LSD in A → End)

0006	58	ASLB	
0007	58	ASLB	
0008	1B	ABA	
0009	D7 34	STAB [34]	Store packed augend
0010	96 32	LDAA [32]	Pack addend
0012	D6 33	LDAB [33]	
0014	58	ASLB	
0015	58	ASLB	
0016	58	ASLB	
0017	58	ASLB	
0018	1B	ABA	Packed addend is now in ACCA
0019	9B 34	ADDA [34]	Add packed augend to ACCA
001B	19	DAA	Correct BCD sum in ACCA
001C	3E	WAI	The end

5. Execute your program by using various BCD numbers. Remember, when entering unpacked BCD numbers into memory, that the most significant nibble is zero.

6. Temporarily replace the DAA instruction with a no-op (NOP) instruction. In 6802 code, the op code for NOP is 01_{16}. Add a few BCD numbers that result in illegal results. This really highlights the usefulness of the DAA instruction.

Part 2

1. It is sometimes necessary to unpack BCD numbers. Unpacking is just as simple as packing. A flowchart that represents the operation is shown in Fig. 8-4. Masking is a term that is applied when certain bits in a byte are placed in known states. For example, if the contents of, say, accumulator A are $1100\ 1101_2$ and we wish to clear the four most significant bits while leaving the four least significant bits unaffected, we logically AND the accumulator with $0000\ 1111_2$. The pattern $0000\ 1111$ is called a mask. That is, $0000\ 1111$ masks off the most significant bits of the 8-bit word.

2. A 6802 program that performs unpacking of a two-digit BCD number is shown below. In this example, the logical AND instruction uses the immediate addressing mode. Direct, indexed, and extended mode addressing also can be used with AND.

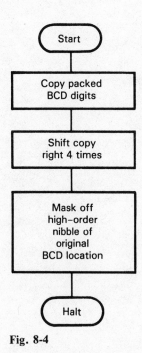

Fig. 8-4

```
0000  96 35   LDAA [35]   ;Load packed BCD digits into ACCA
0002  44      LSRA        ;Shift high-order
0003  44      LSRA        ;  nibble right
0004  44      LSRA        ;  to form
0005  44      LSRA        ;  unpacked MSD
0006  97 36   STAA [36]   ;Store the MSD
0008  96 35   LDAA [35]   ;Reload packed BCD digits into ACCA
000A  84 0F   ANDA# 0F    ;Mask off the high-order nibble
000C  97 37   STAA [37]   ;Store the LSD
000E  3E      WAI         ;The end
```

Program Listing 8-1

3. Enter and execute the unpacking program. You must enter your two packed BCD digits in address location 35_{16} prior to execution. Note also that the unpacked BCD numbers are stored with the MSD in address 0036_{16} and the LSD in address 0037_{16}.

4. Add the unpacking code to the BCD addition program and experiment with various operands.

DISCUSSION TOPICS

Assume that it is necessary to mask the lower nibble of a byte so that the lower half of the byte contains all 1s. How could that be accomplished?

CHAPTER | 9

A Single-Chip 8-bit Microprocessor

ACTIVITY 9-1
TEST: A SINGLE-CHIP
8-BIT MICROPROCESSOR

On a separate sheet of paper, choose the letter that best completes the following statements.

1. The single-chip microprocessor was developed so that microprocessors could be included in _____.
   a. Minicomputers
   b. I/O systems
   c. Low-cost products
   d. Military products

2. A single-chip microprocessor is usually called a(n) _____.
   a. SCM
   b. Microcontroller
   c. Z80
   d. Computer chip

3. This functional block of a computer would not be integrated into a single-chip computer: _____.
   a. Video monitor
   b. ROM
   c. RAM
   d. I/O ports

4. A single-chip microprocessor that is intended for use in battery-powered equipment would most likely be fabricated by using _____.
   a. EPROM
   b. Analog ICs
   c. I/O ports
   d. CMOS

5. The Intel 8051 single-chip microprocessor is similar to the Z80 in that both are _____.
   a. Synchronous devices
   b. General-purpose devices
   c. Register-oriented devices
   d. All of the above

6. The 8051 has the capability to effectively divide memory space into two separate sections for _____.
   a. Serial memory and parallel memory
   b. Program memory and data memory
   c. RAM and registers
   d. Bit-slice operations

7. The 8051 has 22 special-function registers that are located in _____.
   a. Data RAM
   b. ROM
   c. Program RAM
   d. Address locations 0000_{16}–000016_{16}

8. In order to enable the 8051's external memory space, _____.
   a. The serial port must be enabled
   b. The $\overline{EA}$ input must be asserted
   c. Bit instructions must be used
   d. I/O instructions must be used

9. The process whereby a program is transferred from one machine to another is called _____.
   a. Bit-slicing
   b. Parallel I/O
   c. Serial I/O
   d. Downloading

10. The 8052's stack _____.
    a. Is initialized to address 0000_{16}
    b. Grows from low memory toward high memory
    c. Is decremented after any data is pushed
    d. All the above

11. The accumulator of the 8051 is _____.
    a. A 16-bit register
    b. In the scratch-pad section of memory
    c. Bit- or byte-addressable
    d. Not bit-addressable

12. The stack pointer of the 8051 is _____.
    a. A 16-bit register
    b. An 8-bit register
    c. Identical in size and function to that of the Z80
    d. Decremented after data is pushed onto the stack

13. The 8085's data pointer (DPTR) _____.
    a. Is a 16-bit register
    b. Is used to point to locations in external memory
    c. May be accessed as two 8-bit registers
    d. All of the above

14. The 8051 multiplexes the external address bus with _____.
    a. The lower 8 bits of the address bus
    b. The upper 8 bits of the address bus
    c. The full-duplex serial port
    d. Ports 0 and 2

15. When port 0 of the 8051 is read, the input may be taken from the _____.
    a. Actual pin or its associated latch
    b. Internal pull-up
    c. Serial port
    d. ALE pin

16. The 8051 contains two built-in counter-timers. When operated in the counter mode, a given 16-bit counter register is incremented on each
    _____.
    a. Falling edge applied to its T input
    b. Rising edge applied to its T input
    c. High-to-low transition of the internal clock
    d. Machine cycle

17. Two interrupt inputs are available on the 8051. These inputs may be configured to respond in _____.
    a. Either edge- or level-triggered modes
    b. Either transition- or level-triggered modes
    c. Both a and b
    d. Neither a nor b

18. The 8051 contains a section of internal RAM called the scratch-pad memory. The scratch-pad location is found _____.
    a. Beginning at address 0000_{16}
    b. In the I/O space of the processor
    c. Beginning at address $F000_{16}$
    d. In the last 80 bytes of the 8051's internal RAM

19. The 8051's stack pointer can only point to _____.
    a. Internal memory
    b. External RAM
    c. External ROM
    d. An I/O port

20. The 8051 contains a full-duplex, fully buffered _____.
    a. Memory interface
    b. Parallel port
    c. Serial port
    d. Counter-timer

21. 8051 data transfer instructions _____.
    a. Are used in place of arithmetic instructions
    b. Do not affect the state of the status register flags
    c. Are used for serial I/O transfers
    d. Do affect the state of the status register flags

22. When the 8051 performs multiplication and division, operands are located in _____.
    a. The accumulator and the B register
    b. The divisor and dividend registers
    c. Ports 0 and 1
    d. Memory locations

23. Most of the 8051's call and jump instructions use relative addressing. In these cases, the destination address is located relative to either the program counter or the _____.
    a. Index register
    b. Stack pointer
    c. Accumulator
    d. Data pointer

24. The Intel 8052 is the same as an 8051 except that the 8052 contains twice as much ROM and RAM and also contains _____.
    a. An extra parallel port
    b. An extra serial port
    c. An extra 16-bit counter-timer
    d. A built-in color monitor

25. Devices such as the 8052, 8031, and 8032 are often referred to as
_____.
  a. Microcontrollers
  b. Programmable controllers
  c. EPROMs
  d. Application-specific ICs

ACTIVITY 9-2
LAB EXPERIMENT:
CONTROL TRANSFER
INSTRUCTIONS

PURPOSE

This experiment will acquaint you with the operation and typical applications of the commonly used conditional and unconditional control transfer instructions. You will also be introduced to the concept of delay loops and nested loops.

MATERIALS

Qty.
1 Microprocessor trainer
1 Instruction set listing

INTRODUCTION

Control transfer instructions cause program execution to jump from the normal sequence of operation to some other place in a program. The 8051 single-chip microprocessor, as well as all other general-purpose microprocessors, has control transfer instructions. The 6802 has four types of unconditional control transfer instructions: branch always (BRA), branch to subroutine (BSR), jump (JMP), and jump to subroutine (JSR). Jump instructions use extended addressing; branch instructions use 2's complement relative addressing.

There are 15 different conditional control transfer instructions in the 6802's instruction set, and they use only 2's complement relative addressing. An example of such an instruction is branch if equal to zero (BEQ). This instruction causes the program counter of the 6802 to change from its normal sequence if the Z (zero) flag is set. If the Z flag is clear, the branch is not taken.

A subroutine is like a program within a program. A subroutine can be entered at will, and upon completion of the subroutine, program execution will automatically continue from where it left off when the subroutine was called. Recall that a subroutine must end with a return (RET) instruction. Calling a subroutine causes the program counter contents to be pushed onto the stack. When RET is executed, the original contents of the program counter are pulled off the stack. Thus, execution continues where it left off when the subroutine was called.

PROCEDURE

1. One of the simpler and more useful applications of conditional transfer instructions is in the implementation of a delay loop. A delay loop does nothing except use up time. A clock program, for example, would require 1-s delays in order to work properly.

Figure 9-1 illustrates how a delay loop can be structured. This particular structure is called a DO-UNTIL loop. The 6802 machine code for this flowchart is shown below. Here, ACCA is loaded with 05_{16} and repeatedly decremented until it contains 0. Each time the accumulator is decremented, the BNE instruction (branch if not equal to zero) looks at the Z flag. If $Z \neq 1$, the loop is repeated. Note that the relative address is found by counting backward from 1 past the location of the relative address and expressing the distance as a 2's complement number. Load this program and single-step through it. Note how the contents of ACCA are decremented on each pass through the loop.

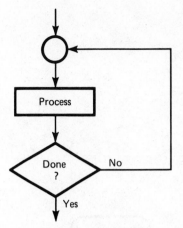

0000	86 05	LDAA# 05	Load ACCA with 05
0002	4A	DECA	Decrement ACCA
0003	26 FD	BNE 02	If ACCA = 00, the branch back −3
0005	3E	WAI	The end, or more code starts here

Fig. 9-1. The DO-UNTIL loop structure.

2. An alternative structure for a delay loop is the DO-WHILE technique shown in Fig. 9-2. A 6802 implementation follows.

0000	86 05	LDAA# 05	Load ACCA with 05
0002	27 03	BEQ 07	If ACCA = 0, branch out of loop (to WAI)
0004	4A	DECA	Decrement ACCA
0005	20 FB	BRA 02	Go back −5 to 0002 and try again
0007	3E	WAI	The end, or more code starts here

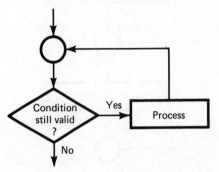

Fig. 9-2. The DO-WHILE loop structure.

Note that this version of the delay loop requires an unconditional branch as well as a conditional branch. Also, the destination of the BEQ instruction cannot be determined until the remaining instructions that make up the loop are written. This is called a forward reference. Load the program and single-step through it. Note how the contents of the accumulator change on each pass through the loop.

3. The amount of time used up by the delay loop is determined primarily by the value initially loaded into ACCA. If we look up the number of machine cycles required for each instruction and we know the time for each machine cycle, the length of the time delay can be determined. By using the DO-UNTIL version of the delay loop, we find that each pass through the loop requires six machine cycles (two for DECA and four for BNE). We won't count initialization of ACCA because it's done only once, regardless of how many times we go through the loop. Anyway, the total delay time is found by multiplying the machine cycles per loop plus 1 by the initial value in ACCA. By using ACCA = 05 and assuming that 1 MPU cycle = 1 μs, we get

$$t_D = 6 \times 6 \ \mu s$$
$$= 36 \ \mu s$$

This is a rather small time delay. The longest delay would occur if ACCA were loaded with FF_{16} (255_{10}):

$$t_D = 256 \times 6 \ \mu s$$
$$= 1.536 \ ms$$

This time delay is proportionately longer, but it might not be long enough for many applications.

4. To increase the time delay, three approaches are possible: First, you

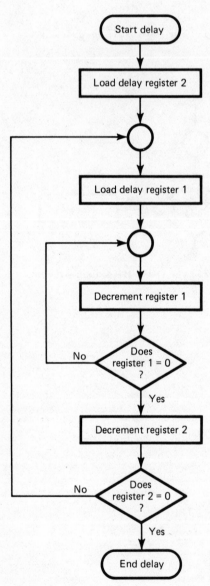

Fig. 9-3

could write several successive delay loops, but that would probably be impractical. For example, by using the DO-UNTIL loop with FF in the accumulator, we would need to rewrite the same delay instructions about 651 times for a 1-s delay.

A second approach would be to use a 16-bit register, such as the IX register, to hold the count. Thus, replacing DECA with DEX results in the use of eight MPU cycles per pass (the DEX instruction uses four MPU cycles as opposed to two for DECA). Initializing to IX = FFFF would produce a delay of $65,536 \times 8 \mu s = 524$ ms. As you can see, that is not really much of an improvement over the use of the accumulator alone.

Finally, the best way to extend delay times is to use nested loops. The flowchart for a time delay using the DO-UNTIL approach and nested loops is shown in Fig. 9-3.

If we assume (arbitrarily) that the inner loop uses an 8-bit register such as ACCA and the outer loop uses a 16-bit register such as IX, it is possible to require as many as $2^8 \times 2^{16} = 16,777,216$ decrement operations to occur before leaving the loop. That would result in a delay time of about 100 s. Delays of hours or days could be achieved by using larger (16-bit) registers and further nesting of loops.

Write the 6802 machine code for the nested delay loop represented by Fig. 9-3.

5. Delay loops are often used as subroutines, and then the delay routine needs to be written only once. Also, such a subroutine may require the calling portion of the program to supply the initial values for the delay time register(s). That allows the delay time to be varied as necessary at different points in the program.

The program listing below uses two subroutines, called OUTBYTE and REDIS, that are stored in ROM on the Heath ET-3600 series microprocessor trainers. When OUTBYTE is called (JSR FE20), the contents of ACCA are displayed as a two-digit hex number. Thus, we have an example of a subroutine that requires the calling program to supply data to the subroutine. The REDIS subroutine resets the display so that, when OUTBYTE is called again, the two hex digits generated are again shown in the left-most displays. The function of this program is to count from 0 to FF_{16} over and over again while displaying the count in the left-most seven-segment displays. The program also incorporates a delay loop that uses the index register as a counter. The delay loop is not a subroutine in this program.

Load and execute the program. Experiment with different values in the index register, and note the effect on the counting speed.

```
0000  4F          CLRA          Clear ACCA
0001  CE FF FF     LDX# FFFF     Load FFFF into IX
0004  09          DEX           Decrement IX
0005  26 FD        BNE 04        If IX ≠ 0, go back to
                                 0004
0007  BD FE 20     JSR FE20      Jump to OUTBYTE
                                 subroutine (Dis-
                                 play ACCA)
000A  4C          INCA          Increment ACCA for
                                 next number to
                                 display
000B  BD FC BC     JSR FCBC      Jump to REDIS sub-
                                 routine
000E  20 F1        BRA 01        Branch back to 0001
                                 and go again
```

58

CHAPTER | 10

Sixteen-Bit Microprocessors: The 8088 and the 68000

ACTIVITY 10-1
TEST: SIXTEEN-BIT
MICROPROCESSORS: THE 8088
AND THE 68000

On a separate sheet of paper, choose the answer that best fits the following questions and statements.

1. Structurally, the 8088 and the 8086 are similar except that the 8088 has a(n) _____ external data bus and the 8086 has a(n) _____ external data bus.
   a. Tristate, TTL
   b. 8-bit, 16-bit
   c. 16-bit, 8-bit
   d. None of the above

2. Sixteen- and thirty-two-bit microprocessors were developed _____.
   a. To provide increased computational power for microcomputers
   b. To increase processing speed
   c. To be used in applications where 8-bit microprocessors are not powerful enough.
   d. All of the above

3. Which of the following would probably not contain a 68000 microprocessor? _____
   a. An engineering workstation
   b. A graphics processor
   c. A fancy toaster
   d. An Apple Macintosh

4. The Intel 8088 and 8086 microprocessors use a form of addressing in which op codes are located in reference to the contents of the _____ register.
   a. Code segment
   b. Data segment
   c. Extra segment
   d. Stack segment

5. The 8088 is capable of fetching op codes while it is executing instructions. Such prefetched op codes are stored in the _____.
   a. Instruction pointer
   b. Instruction stream queue
   c. Extra segment register
   d. Base pointer

6. The 8088 and 8086 have _____ -bit address buses.
   a. 8
   b. 16
   c. 20
   d. 32

7. The 8088 and 8086 use isolated I/O, thereby providing I/O addresses that range from 0000_{16} to $FFFF_{16}$. How many address lines does this require? _____
   a. 8
   b. 16
   c. 20
   d. 32

8. When an address is formed by an 8088 or 8086, the contents of the appropriate segment register are effectively _____ before they are added to the 16-bit address provided by the instruction being executed.
   a. Shifted left by 4 bits
   b. Multiplied by 16_{10}
   c. Multiplied by 10_{16}
   d. All of the above

9. The 8088/8086 segment registers are used to divide memory into blocks that are _____ bytes long.
   a. 16
   b. 64K
   c. 2^{20}
   d. None of the above

10. The 8088/8086 register that is equivalent to the program counter in the 6800 microprocessor is the _____.
    a. Code segment register
    b. Data segment register
    c. Instruction pointer
    d. Destination index

11. The 8088/8086 direction flag (DF), interrupt flag (IF), and trap flag (TF) are referred to as _____ flags.
    a. General-purpose
    b. Control
    c. Prefetch
    d. Physical address

12. The 8088/8086 contains four general-purpose registers called AX, BX, CX, and DX. These registers are _____.
    a. 8 bits wide
    b. 16 bits wide
    c. 32 bits wide
    d. 20 bits wide

13. When a given 8088/8086 instruction does not specify in which segment an indirectly addressed operand is located, the default location is within the _____.
    a. Current code segment
    b. Current data segment
    c. Current stack segment
    d. I/O address space

14. To force the 8088/8086 to fetch an operand from the extra segment address space, _____ must be placed before the instruction that is to access the data.
    a. The ES segment override prefix
    b. The CS segment override prefix
    c. A MOD field
    d. An R/M field

15. This type of 8088/8086 instruction has no direct equivalent in 6802 machine code: _____.
    a. MOV
    b. POP
    c. ADD
    d. SAR

16. The 8088/8086 _____ instruction would be used to perform multiplication of unsigned operands.
    a. MUL   *c.* DAA
    b. IMUL   *d.* DAS

17. 8088/8086 conditional transfers such as JGE/JNL can be used only _____.
    a. In the relative addressing mode
    b. For intersegment jumps
    c. In page 0 of memory
    d. For none of the above

18. A jump (in an 8088/8086 system) that causes execution of code that is outside the current code segment is _____.
    a. An intersegment jump
    b. An intrasegment jump
    c. Not possible
    d. A conditional transfer instruction

19. The LOOPNZ instruction loops _____.
    a. Until the CX register contains zero
    b. Until the CX register does not contain zero
    c. Until the CF flag is set
    d. If CX is not zero and the CF flag is clear

20. When an 8088 interrupt is acknowledged, the interrupting device or an interrupt controller must _____.
    a. Execute a segment override prefix
    b. Execute an SCAS instruction
    c. Supply an interrupt type number
    d. Supply an interrupt vector

21. The 8088 external data bus is _____.
    a. 16 bits wide
    b. Multiplexed with the address bus
    c. Latched internally in the 8088
    d. Taken from the bus controller output lines

22. An 8088 or 8086, when configured in the maximum mode, _____.
    a. Requires an external bus controller
    b. Generates its own internal clock
    c. Requires fewer support devices than the minimum mode requires
    d. Does not require buffering of the data bus.

23. The Motorola 68000 address bus is _____ bits wide.
    a. 16   *c.* 23
    b. 20   *d.* 32

24. The 68000's data bus is _____ bits wide.
   a. 8   *c.* 20
   b. 16   *d.* 23

25. The least significant bit of the 68000 address bus (A_0) is used _____.

   a. In the same way as by the 8088
   b. As a carry flag
   c. To select even and odd bytes of data words
   d. To access only long-word data

26. The 68000 has _____ stack pointer(s).
   a. 1   *c.* 8
   b. 2   *d.* 17

27. The 68000 has two privileged states of operation. They are _____.

   a. User and supervisor
   b. Controller and server
   c. Sequential and combinational
   d. Maskable and nonmaskable

28. The 68000 has three major processing states: normal processing, exception processing, and _____.
   a. Supervisor processing
   b. Trace processing
   c. Register processing
   d. Halt processing

29. All of the 68000's seventeen 32-bit registers can be used as _____.

   a. Index registers
   b. Stack pointers
   c. Effective address registers
   d. Program counters

30. In the long-addressing mode, the address of a given operand is contained in _____.
   a. Two bytes following the op code
   b. The index register
   c. Two 16-bit words following the op code
   d. A signed 2's complement byte following the op code

31. One of the more unique features of the 68000 is that its buses are _____.

   a. Serial
   b. Synchronous
   c. Asynchronous
   d. Always on time

32. Unlike the 6802, the 68000 requires an interrupting device to supply a(n) _____.
   a. 8-bit interrupt vector
   b. 24-bit interrupt vector
   c. Interrupt priority mask
   d. RTE instruction

33. The 68000 uses two different kinds of relative addressing. One type adds a 16-bit offset to the program counter. The second type adds an 8-bit offset and _____ to the program counter.
   a. An interrupt vector
   b. A supervisor mode flag
   c. The contents of an index register
   d. The contents of the stack pointer

34. The equivalent of a nonmaskable interrupt on the 68000 is _____.

    a. Priority level 0

    b. Priority level 7

    c. Priority level 8

    d. None of the above; there is no such interrupt on the 68000

35. When an interrupt is initiated, the 68000 enters the _____.

    a. Halt processing state

    b. Normal processing state

    c. Exception processing state

    d. BCD processing state

ACTIVITY 10-2
LAB EXPERIMENT:
AN 8088 DEBUGGER

PURPOSE

Debuggers are programs that allow the microcomputer user to easily examine and modify the contents of the machine's registers and memory. In this experiment, you will be familiarized with the debugger that is used with 8088-based machines such as the IBM PC and its relatives. You will also gain experience with the structure of the 8088 instructions.

MATERIALS

Qty.

1 IBM AT, IBM XT, or an equivalent machine

1 Disk operating system: MS-DOS, IBM PC-DOS, or equivalent

1 Supplemental DOS (contains the debugger program DEBUG.COM)

INTRODUCTION

Up to this point, it is more than likely that you have been entering programs into your trainer strictly in hexadecimal form. Of course, you would write a program in mnemonic form first for your own convenience. More sophisticated systems, such as the IBM PC, also include provisions for directly manipulating memory and register contents just as simple microprocessor trainers do. These capabilities are provided by a debugger program.

Debuggers also usually allow the user to enter instructions into memory in mnemonic form. That is fortunate, considering the complexity of op code construction for the 8088 microprocessor. Debuggers allow the contents of memory to be displayed in both numerical and ASCII forms. Also, when machine language programs are being entered, the debugger will automatically determine the correct 2's complement address for instructions that use relative addressing.

In this experiment, you will use a program called DEBUG to examine and enter data and instructions into the microcomputer. Examples of many of the 8088 instructions will be examined.

PROCEDURE

Part 1

1. Insert the DOS disk in drive A and then close the door of the disk drive as shown in Fig. 10-1.

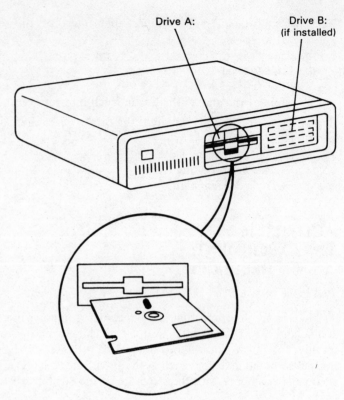

Drive A:

Drive B:
(if installed)

Fig. 10-1. Insert disk in drive A: as shown here.

2. Turn on the computer and the monitor if necessary. After a minute or so, the computer should beep and ask for the date. You can either enter the date or just press return or enter to skip the date. Next you will be asked for the time. You can enter the time or skip this question as well. At this point you should see the DOS prompt A⟩.

3. Remove the DOS disk and replace it with the supplemental DOS disk that contains the debugger program. Verify that DEBUG.COM is on the disk by typing and entering DIR. That causes a list of the files on the disk to be printed out. DEBUG.COM should be somewhere in the list.

4. Now, to run the debugger, just type DEBUG and press return. Note that you may use uppercase or lowercase letters or a combination; it does not matter here. The DEBUG prompt should now be seen on the screen.

5. Let's take a look at the contents of the registers. To do so, enter the letter R. This causes a register dump; i.e., the contents of the registers are dumped to the screen. Your display should be similar to that shown in Fig. 10-2, but most of your actual contents will probably be different.

6. Most of the register dump display is self-explanatory. For example, in Fig. 10-2, the first 13 equalities are just the 8088's registers and their hex contents. Following these registers are the status flags, which are decoded as shown in Fig. 10-3. The last row of Fig. 10-

```
-r
AX=0000  BX=0000 CX=0000 DX=0000  SP=FFEE BP=0000  SI=0000  DI=0000
DS=090F  ES=090F SS=090F CS=090F  IP=0100   NV UP DI PL NZ NA PO NC
090F:0100 0A750C      OR      DH,[DI+0C]                  DS:000C=1E
-
```

Fig. 10-2

Flag	Name	Set	Clear
OF	Overflow	OV	NV
DF	Direction	DN	UP
IF	Interrupt	EI	DI
SF	Sign	NG	PL
ZF	Zero	ZR	NZ
AF	Aux. carry	AC	NA
PF	Parity	PE	PO
CF	Carry	CY	NC

Fig. 10-3

2 begins with 090F:0100, which is the code for the physical address of the first instruction in line for execution. The four-digit hex number to the left of the colon is the segment address (code segment CS). The four-digit number to the right of the colon is the instruction pointer contents.

Following the address in Fig. 10-2 is the hex number 0A750C, which is the op code for the instruction OR DH, [DI+0C]. It means "Logically OR the contents of the DH register with the contents of the memory location pointed to by the sum of the DI register plus an offset (8-bit) of 0C and store the result in DH." That's quite an instruction, but it's typical of the instructions used in 8088 programs.

The final entry in Fig. 10-2 is DS:000C = 1E, which tells us that the contents of memory location 000C in the data segment are 1E.

7. You may change the contents of a given register by entering the two-digit code for that register. For example, to change the contents of the CX register to $ABCD_{16}$, type and enter RCX. You should see the current contents of CX displayed, and below this a colon is printed. Type the new contents of CX (ABCD) and press return. A register dump will now verify that CX has been changed.

8. The contents of memory can be examined by using the D (dump) command. For example, if we enter D 100, a display like that of Fig. 10-4 will be produced. Because a segment value was not specified, the memory contents displayed are those starting at offset 100_{16} in the current data segment. The default dump length is 80_{16} memory locations (from offset 100_{16} to offset 180_{16} in Fig. 10-4). Enter D 100 and verify this operation.

Note that the hex contents of the memory are shown in the left three-fourths of the screen and the right edge of the screen shows

```
-d100
090F:0100  0A 75 0C FF 06 44 19 C7-06 42 19 00 00 EB 18 8B   .u...D.G.B...k..
090F:0110  46 06 8B 76 04 03 76 0A-8E C0 26 8A 1C 30 FF 53   F..v..v..a&..0.S
090F:0120  9A 3C 02 7C 0A 8B E5 FF-46 0A EB B3 8B 46 06 8B   .<.:..e.F.k3.F..
090F:0130  5E 04 3B 06 D4 2D 75 04-3B 1E D2 2D 75 33 9A 73   ^.;.T-u.;.R-u3.s
090F:0140  02 7C 0A 9A 31 1F 44 06-3D 1B 00 89 46 0A 74 0E   .:..1.D.=...F.t.
090F:0150  3D 0D 00 75 02 EB 07 9A-0E 00 7B 0A EB E5 C7 06   =..u.k....{.keG.
090F:0160  06 29 00 00 83 7E 0A 1B-75 11 C7 46 08 02 00 EB   .)...~..u.GF...k
090F:0170  0A B8 01 00 50 0E E8 9C-FD 8B E5 0E E8 08 00 8B   .8..P.h.}.e.h...
-
```

Fig. 10-4

the ASCII code representation of each byte. When a byte does not represent a valid ASCII code, a period is printed.

9. You may change the contents of a contiguous block of memory by using the F (fill) command. For example, enter the command

$$F\ 100,170,AA$$

where F is the fill command, 100 is the offset of the start of the block of memory, 170 is the offset of the end of the block, and AA is the hex value to fill in the block. Verify that this command functions as described by dumping the modified memory contents.

10. If necessary, the contents of any memory location can be examined by entering a complete address with the memory dump command. For example, to see what's in the very beginning of memory, enter

$$D\ 0000:0000$$

This is where the 8088 interrupt vectors are located.

Part 2

1. The debugger program allows you to enter and examine programs in mnemonic form. The U (unassemble) command causes the hex op codes and mnemonics for a program to be shown. For example, enter the following command:

$$U\ 200,230$$

You should see a display similar to that of Fig. 10-5. This is a listing of the contents of memory in the current code segment starting at offset 200_{16} and ending with the last complete instruction that has a byte in offset 230_{16}. Keep in mind that we are looking at essentially random code, and your display will probably consist of instructions completely different from those in Fig. 10-5.

2. If you just type U, unassembly (or disassembly, as it is usually called) will continue from where it left off previously. Try this a few times to get a feel for the command.

3. You can unassemble any section of code by supplying a complete address specification. The format is

$$U\ SSSS:XXXX,YYYY$$

where SSSS is the code segment value, XXXX is the starting offset, and YYYY is the ending offset.

4. Now let's look at a way to assemble programs in mnemonic form. Program assembly is begun by using the A (assemble) command. Start assembly at offset 0100_{16} of the code segment by entering A 100.

5. We will now enter the mnemonics for the instruction that will move the contents of the AX register into the BX register by typing

$$MOV\ BX,AX$$

and then pressing return. The debugger will automatically enter the correct op code into memory.

6. Write down the 8088 mnemonics for the following operations.
   a. Transfer contents of CX into DX.
   b. Transfer the contents of the memory location pointed to by the SI register into the AL register.
   c. Decrement the CX register.
   d. Transfer the contents of the AH register into the memory location pointed to by the DI register plus a constant offset of $A2_{16}$.
   e. Add the number $F0_{16}$ to the CL register.
   f. Logically AND the contents of the AH register with the contents of the memory location at offset $4C_{16}$ and have the result stored in location $4C_{16}$.
   g. Execute interrupt 20_{16}.

```
-u200,230
090F:0200 7C0A        JL    020C
090F:0202 9A05008C09  CALL  098C:0005
090F:0207 85C0         TEST  AX,AX
090F:0209 74F7         JZ    0202
090F:020B 9A311F4406  CALL  0644:1F31
090F:0210 83C402       ADD   SP,+02
090F:0213 5D           POP   BP
090F:0214 CB           RETF
090F:0215 55           PUSH  BP
090F:0216 83EC02       SUB   SP,+02
090F:0219 8BEC         MOV   BP,SP
090F:021B 33C0         XOR   AX,AX
090F:021D 50           PUSH  AX
090F:021E 33C0         XOR   AX,AX
090F:0220 50           PUSH  AX
090F:0221 33DB         XOR   BX,BX
090F:0223 53           PUSH  BX
090F:0224 1E           PUSH  DS
090F:0225 B83A0D       MOV   AX,0D3A
090F:0228 50           PUSH  AX
090F:0229 9A0F00C009  CALL  09C0:000F
090F:022E 8BE5         MOV   SP,BP
090F:0230 83C402       ADD   SP,+02
-
```

Fig. 10-5

7. To see if you wrote down the correct mnemonics, enter them into the machine by using the command

A 100

Illegal or nonsense mnemonics will be rejected.

8. Unassemble the instructions you just entered. Note that the debugger has filled in the hex op codes as required.

9. Many more features are available in DEBUG than we have time to explore, so, for now, try experimenting with the entry of various mnemonic expressions into the machine.

CHAPTER | 11

Memory

On a separate sheet of paper, choose the answer that best fits the following statements and questions.

1. The most commonly used microprocessor memory technology is

   _____.
   a. Core technology
   b. Bipolar transistor
   c. MOS transistor
   d. Charge-coupled device

2. Static memory devices store data in _____.
   a. Flip-flops
   b. Magnetic cores
   c. Gates
   d. Capacitors

3. An example of a typical mass storage device is _____.
   a. A bipolar RAM
   b. A static RAM
   c. A dynamic RAM
   d. Magnetic tape

4. The time required for data to be written into a memory is called

   _____.
   a. Read access time
   b. Cycle time
   c. Propagation delay time
   d. Sequential access time

5. _____ is an example of nonvolatile memory.
   a. Static RAM
   b. Dynamic RAM
   c. The floppy disk
   d. SRAM

6. A bootstrap or boot program is normally located in _____.
   a. RAM   c. Interrupt vector tables
   b. ROM   d. Sequential access memory

7. This type of memory provides very fast access: _____.
   a. MOS memory
   b. Bipolar memory
   c. Sequential access memory
   d. Magnetic tape

8. This type of memory requires periodic refreshing of its contents: _____.
   a. Static RAM
   b. Dynamic RAM
   c. Mask-programmed ROM
   d. EPROM

9. Memory devices constructed by using _____ technology generally have very low power dissipation.
   a. NMOS
   b. PMOS
   c. CMOS
   d. Bipolar

10. In static RAMs, a given bit of data is stored in _____.
    a. A flip-flop
    b. A capacitor
    c. A shift register
    d. Magnetic domains

11. A certain memory chip is described as being a 2K × 4 DRAM. How many storage cells will this device contain? _____
    a. 2000
    b. 2048
    c. 8000
    d. 8192

12. How many address pins will a nonmultiplexed 4K × 1 DRAM have? _____
    a. 8
    b. 11
    c. 12
    d. 13

13. A certain 64K × 1 DRAM uses multiplexed addressing. How many address lines are required by this device? _____
    a. 7
    b. 8
    c. 16
    d. 1

14. Generally speaking, a given memory device is enabled for read or write operation when _____ is asserted.
    a. Chip select
    b. CAS
    c. RAS
    d. R/$\overline{\text{W}}$

15. Errors or loss of data in memory chips is often detected by using _____.
    a. Johnson counters
    b. Refresh counters
    c. Parity checking
    d. Parallel processors

16. In the _____ memory technology, the manufacturer must program the ROM during the fabrication process.
    a. EAROM
    b. EPROM
    c. Fusible-link ROM
    d. Mask-programmed ROM

17. I/O applications that require extremely fast access to memory would use this technique: _____.
    a. Polling
    b. DMA
    c. Paging
    d. Bank switching

18. Normally, a microprocessor with a 16-bit address bus could address a maximum of 64K memory locations. However, _____ allows this range to be increased.
    a. Bank switching
    b. DMA
    c. Parallel I/O
    d. Memory-mapped I/O

19. Multiplexed addressing is used in the construction of RAMs for this reason: _____.
    a. To confuse RAM users
    b. To reduce pin count
    c. To decrease access time
    d. To allow for bank switching

20. The standardized form of bank switching used in IBM PC and compatible systems is called _____.
    a. Segmented addressing
    b. EMS
    c. EMT
    d. CPR

21. EPROMs are erased by _____.
    a. Exposure to infrared radiation
    b. Exposure to cold
    c. Exposure to ultraviolet radiation
    d. Application of refresh signals

ACTIVITY 11-2
LAB EXPERIMENT:
MEMORY TEST PROGRAMS

PURPOSE

In this experiment you will work with several programs that can be used to test the system's memory devices. Simple programs to clear and set memory locations and a more sophisticated program called a rolling memory test will be presented. Also, the use of registers as counters is explored further.

MATERIALS

Qty.
1   Microprocessor trainer or IBM PC (or compatible)
1   Instruction set listing

INTRODUCTION

At first, memory testing might seem to be a simple task. That seems especially true when you have a microprocessor to run the test. For example, you could execute a program that writes all 0s into each word. After all 0s were written, the program could then read each location and check for the presence of all 0s. The test would determine if any locations were stuck high. In a similar manner, we could then run a program that loads all 1s into each location, reads back each location, and detects any bits that are stuck low.

This all 0s, all 1s type of testing is relatively simple, but it does not catch some other somewhat less frequently occurring problems with memories. For example, sometimes a memory may exhibit pattern-sensitive errors. Pattern sensitivity means that the state of a given bit depends on the states of the bits around it, rather than what was originally stored in it.

There are many tests that will detect pattern-sensitive errors. One common and rather simple test is the rolling memory test. This test rolls through memory from a given starting address to a stop address, writing then reading and testing, for each possible binary pattern from all 0s to all 1s. This test ensures that each location is tested with all possible bit patterns that could be stored. Sensitivity to contents of neighboring memory locations is not tested, however, and this leads to even more sophisticated test procedures.

You will begin this experiment with the simple memory test, and then the rolling memory test will be investigated.

PROCEDURE

Part 1

1. Refer to the flowchart in Fig. 11-1. Note that no microprocessor-specific registers are given. This is a generalized flowchart, and the details of which registers are used are up to the programmer. An implementation of this flowchart in 6802 machine code is shown in Listing 11-1. There the index register (IX) is the memory pointer and the counter. The starting address of the beginning of the test memory is the offset used in the load and store accumulator A (indexed addressing) instructions. The test pattern stored first (00_{16}) is held in ACCA. After the test pattern is moved from ACCA into memory, the pattern is loaded back into ACCB, which is then compared to ACCA. If there is a match, execution continues with the test of the next location. If there is a mismatch, the error flag location (address 0030_{16}) is set to 01_{16}, and then the program terminates. This program will test memory locations 0050_{16} through $005F_{16}$. The parameters can be changed by changing the index offset (50_{16}) and the immediate operand of the CPX instruction ($000F_{16}$). If you are using a 6802-based trainer, enter this program.

```
0000 6F 00 30   CLR  [0030]      ;Clear the error flag (extended mode)
0003 CE 00 00   LDX# 0000        ;Initialize memory pointer
0006 4F         CLRA             ;Clear test pattern register
0007 A7 50      STAA [IX+50]     ;Store test pattern
0009 E6 50      LDAB [IX+50]     ;Read test pattern
000B 11         CBA              ;Read pattern = stored pattern?
000C 26 10      BNE  1F          ;If no, goto error routine at 001F
000E 43         COMA             ;Invert (complement) test pattern
000F A7 50      STAA [IX+50]     ;Store inverted test pattern
0011 E6 50      LDAB [IX+50]     ;Read back inverted test pattern
0013 11         CBA              ;Read pattern = stored pattern?
0014 26 08      BNE  1F          ;If no, goto error routine at 001F
0016 8C 00 0F   CPX# 000F        ;Last location tested yet?
0019 27 06      BEQ  22          ;If yes, goto WAI at 0022
001C 08         INX              ;Increment memory pointer
001D 20 E8      BRA  06          ;Go back to 0006 and run test again
001F 7C 00 30   INC  [0030]      ;Increment error flag (extended)
0022 3E         WAI              ;The end
```

Program Listing 11-1

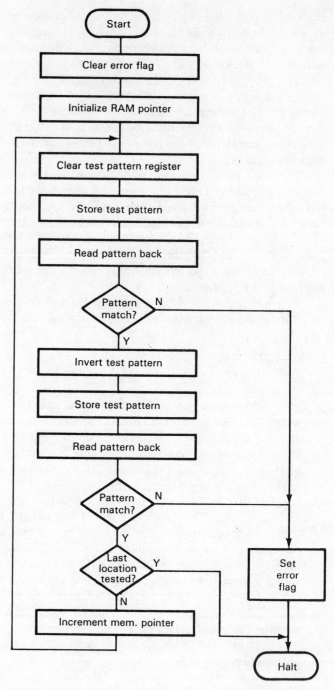

Fig. 11-1

2. An 8088 version of the flowchart is shown in Listing 11-2. If you are using an IBM AT, IBM XT, or a compatible computer, load DEBUG and assemble this code. In this example, memory locations XXXX:0200 through XXXX:020F are tested. Remember, your segment address (XXXX) is set by DEBUG when it is executed, and it will probably differ from the segment address shown in this listing.

3. Whichever system you are using, single-step through the program once to be sure that the program works properly. If you are using DEBUG, you must ensure that the IP register is set to 0100. To do so, enter rip

```
-A100
090F:0100 MOV CX,0000         ;Clear error counter
090F:0103 MOV DI,0000         ;Initialize test RAM pointer
090F:0106 MOV AL,00           ;Clear test pattern register
090F:0108 MOV [DI+0200],AL    ;Store test pattern
090F:010C MOV BL,[DI+0200]    ;Read back test pattern
090F:0110 CMP AL,BL           ;Stored pattern = read pattern?
090F:0112 JNZ 012B            ;If no, jump to error flag
090F:0114 NOT AL              ;Invert test pattern
090F:0116 MOV [DI+0200],AL    ;Store inverted pattern
090F:011A MOV BL,[DI+0200]    ;Read back pattern
090F:011E CMP AL,BL           ;Stored pattern = read pattern?
090F:0120 JNZ 012A            ;If no, jump to error flag
090F:0122 CMP DI,+0F          ;Last location tested?
090F:0126 JZ 012C             ;If yes, jump to the end
090F:0128 INC DI              ;Increment memory pointer
090F:0129 JMP 0106            ;Go back and test again
090F:012B INC CX              ;Increment error flag
090F:012C INT 20              ;The End
090F:012E
-
```

Program Listing 11-2

at the prompt. If DEBUG responds with :0100, just press return; otherwise, enter 0100. That is shown in the first three lines of Fig. 11-2. Now, repeatedly enter t (for trace) to single-step. Every time you enter t, the registers will dump to the screen, and the next instruction to be executed will be printed. That also is shown in Fig. 11-2.

IMPORTANT: Single-step only until the IP points to INT 20. Do not single-step beyond that point.

4. If you are sure the program works properly, single-step to the point where the pattern comparison is made (CBA in the 6802 listing and CMP AL,BL in the DEBUG listing). When you reach that point, change the contents of ACCB or the BX register so that pattern match does not occur. (In DEBUG, that is done by entering RBX and then entering the desired wrong number. You cannot directly specify the BL register by using the DEBUG r command.) The process is shown in Fig. 11-3.

5. Execute the program normally this time. If you are using DEBUG,

```
-rip
IP 0103
:0100
-t

AX=0000 BX=0000 CX=0000 DX=0000 SP=FFEE BP=0000 SI=0000 DI=0000
DS=090F ES=090F SS=090F CS=090F IP=0103   NV UP DI NG NZ AC PE CY
090F:0103 BF0000          MOV     DI,0000
-t

AX=0000 BX=0000 CX=0000 DX=0000 SP=FFEE BP=0000 SI=0000 DI=0000
DS=090F ES=090F SS=090F CS=090F IP=0106   NV UP DI NG NZ AC PE CY
090F:0106 B000           MOV     AL,00
-t

AX=0000 BX=0000 CX=0000 DX=0000 SP=FFEE BP=0000 SI=0000 DI=0000
DS=090F ES=090F SS=090F CS=090F IP=0108   NV UP DI NG NZ AC PE CY
090F:0108 88850002       MOV     [DI+0200],AL             DS:0200=00
-t

AX=0000 BX=0000 CX=0000 DX=0000 SP=FFEE BP=0000 SI=0000 DI=0000
DS=090F ES=090F SS=090F CS=090F IP=010C   NV UP DI NG NZ AC PE CY
090F:010C 8A9D0002       MOV     BL,[DI+0200]             DS:0200=00
-
```

Fig. 11-2

```
AX=0000 BX=0000 CX=0000 DX=0000 SP=FFEE BP=0000 SI=0000 DI=0000
DS=090F ES=090F SS=090F CS=090F IP=0110  NV UP DI NG NZ AC PE CY
090F:0110 38D8          CMP     AL,BL
-rbx
BX 0000
:0001
-t

AX=0000 BX=0001 CX=0000 DX=0000 SP=FFEE BP=0000 SI=0000 DI=0000
DS=090F ES=090F SS=090F CS=090F IP=0112  NV UP DI NG NZ AC PE CY
090F:0112 7511          JNZ     0128
-t
```

Fig. 11-3

you should enter the starting address of the program into the IP register and then enter G (for GO). This sequence of keystrokes is:

```
rip        Tell DEBUG to display contents of IP
IP XXXX Current contents of IP
:0100      You enter the starting address 0100
g          Now you enter g to execute the program
           The computer responds with ''Program
           terminated normally''
```

6. Verify that the test RAM is error-free. On 6802-based systems, you examine location 0030 and verify that it contains 00_{16}. On the PC, dump the registers or just examine the CX register.

```
0000 6F 00 30    CLR  [0030]    ;Clear error flag
0003 CE 00 00    LDX# 0000      ;Initialize memory pointer
0006 4F          CLRA           ;Clear test pattern register
0007 A7 50       STAA [IX+50]   ;Store test pattern
0009 E6 50       LDAB [IX+50]   ;Read test pattern
000B 11          CBA            ;Compare stored and read pattern
000C 26 0F       BNE  1D        ;If not equal, inc. error flag
000E 81 FF       CMPA# FF       ;Last pattern tested yet?
0010 27 03       BEQ  15        ;If yes, then goto addr. 0015
0012 4C          INCA           ;If no, increment pattern
0013 20 F2       BRA  07        ;and run test again
0015 8C 00 0F    CPX# 000F      ;Last location tested yet?
0018 27 06       BEQ  20        ;If yes, then goto the end
001A 08          INX            ;Increment memory pointer
001B 20 E9       BRA  06        ;Go back and test next location
001D 7C 00 30    INC  [0030]    ;Set the error flag
0020 3E          WAI            ;The end
```

Program Listing 11-3

```
-A100
090F:0100 MOV CX,0000         ;Clear error flag
090F:0103 MOV DI,0000         ;Initialize test memory pointer
090F:0106 MOV AL,00           ;Clear test pattern register
090F:0108 MOV [DI+0200],AL    ;Store test pattern
090F:010C MOV BL,[DI+0200]    ;Read back test pattern
090F:0110 CMP AL,BL           ;Are patterns the same?
090F:0112 JNZ 0125            ;If no, jump to error flag
090F:0114 CMP AL,FF           ;Last pattern tried?
090F:0116 JZ 011C             ;If yes, then goto 011C
090F:0118 INC AL              ;Increment test pattern
090F:011A JMP 0108            ;Goto 0108 and test next location
090F:011C CMP DI,+0F          ;Last memory location tested?
090F:0120 JZ 0125             ;If yes, goto the end
090F:0122 INC DI              ;Increment memory pointer
090F:0123 JMP 0106            ;Go back and run test again
090F:0125 INC CX              ;Set the error flag
090F:0126 INT 20              ;The end
090F:0128
-
```

Program Listing 11-4

Part 2

1. The flowchart in Fig. 11-4 represents the rolling memory test. Listing 11-3 shows the 6802 code for this test, and Listing 11-4 is the 8088 code. Enter the appropriate program into your machine.
2. Even though we are testing only 16 memory locations, it would be impractical to single-step through the entire program because each location is tested with 256 different patterns. Use Part 1 as a guide to devise your own procedure for checking program operation.

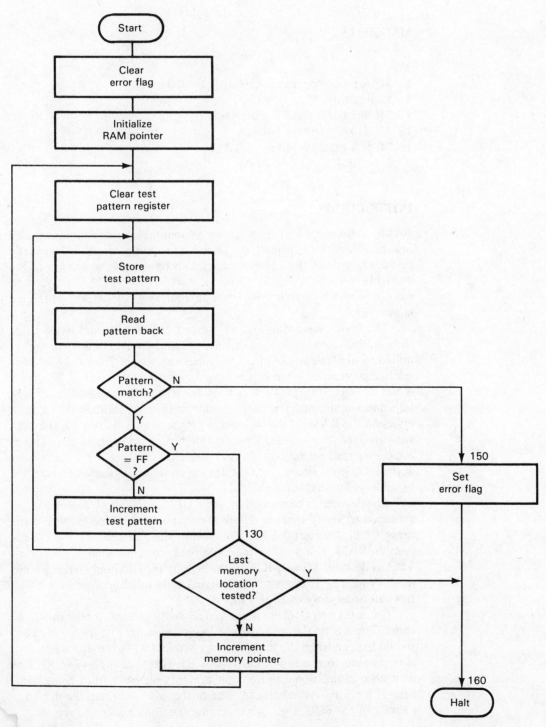

Fig. 11-4

ACTIVITY 11-3
LAB EXPERIMENT:
EXPANDING MEMORY ON THE
MICROPROCESSOR TRAINER

PURPOSE

In this experiment you will expand the RAM of your microprocessor trainer. The operation of address-decoding circuitry will be examined and tested by using a logic probe. The expansion memory will be tested by using manual and programmed test techniques.

MATERIALS

Qty.

1 Microprocessor trainer (Heath ET-3400 type)
1 Logic probe
1 74LS27 triple three-input NOR
1 74LS30 eight-input NAND
1 74LS08 quad two-input AND
2 2114 1024 × 4 static RAM

INTRODUCTION

Adding memory to a microprocessor system means more than just adding the RAM chips themselves. Decoding circuitry also must normally be added; it maps the added memory into one particular section of the available memory space. In addition, it allows the RAM to respond to read or write commands only when an address within its mapped range is asserted.

The logic diagram in Fig. 11-5 shows the decoder and RAM chips to be added to the trainer in this experiment. Two 2114 devices are required to implement a byte-oriented memory space. The 2114 SRAM is selected or enabled when its $\overline{CS}$ input is asserted (active low). When $\overline{CS}$ is not asserted, the 2114's I/O lines are tristated, or placed in a high-impedance state, and the state of address lines A_0 through A_9 have no effect on the RAM. If the $\overline{W}$ input is high while CS is asserted, the 2114 will drive the data selected by A_0 through A_9 onto the data bus. This is a memory-read operation. If CS is asserted and $\overline{W}$ is low, data present at the I/O pins is latched into the 2114 at an internal location determined by address lines A_0 through A_9.

The decoder is comprised of gates U1A, U1B, and U2. You are encouraged to verify that the 2114s are enabled for addresses within the range 0400_{16} through $07FF_{16}$. This means that, in order to use the expansion RAM, you must write to and read from this span of addresses. VMA is decoded because it is driven high by the CPU only when a valid memory address is present. Clock signal is decoded because data transfers can occur only when this line is high.

Gates U3 and U1C are needed to allow the trainer to read the RAM chips. The RE line must be driven low to pass data to the CPU. That should happen when the RAM is addressed and R/$\overline{W}$ is high. When data is being sent to the expansion RAM, $\overline{RE}$ is driven high. The $\overline{RE}$ line controls a bidirectional buffer that prevents the 6802 from being damaged if a wiring error is made. The buffer also increases the drive capability of the 6802, thereby preventing data bus loading problems.

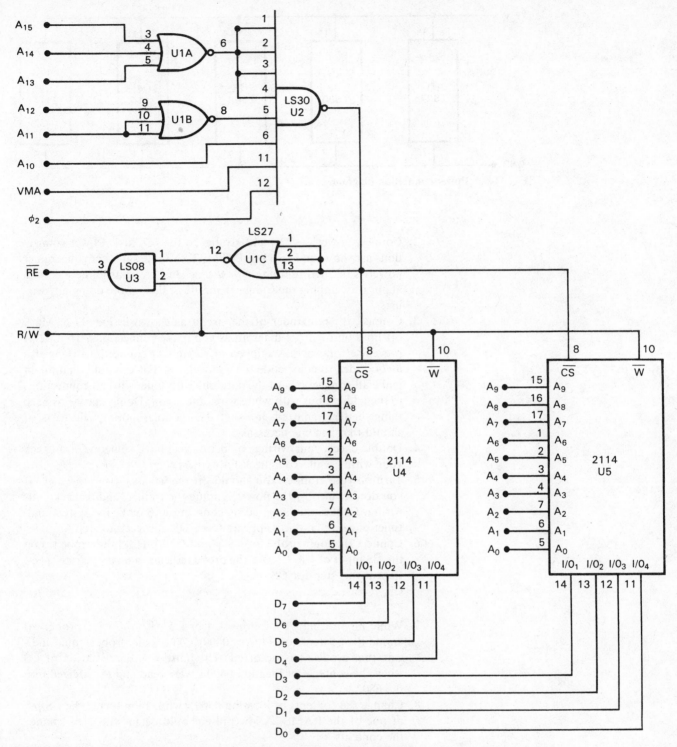

Fig. 11-5. A 1-kilobyte memory expansion using 2114 1024 × 4 static RAMs.

PROCEDURE

1. Insert U1 through U5 in the breadboard of your trainer. Because the 2114s are MOS devices, it is a good idea to touch a grounded object such as a water pipe before handling them. That will drain off any large electric charge that you may have built up. Handle the 2114s only when necessary, and keep them in their conductive foam whenever possible.

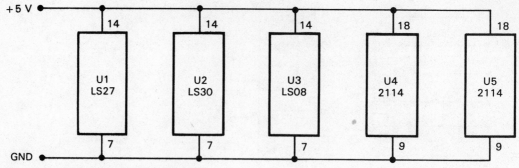

Fig. 11-6. Power connection diagram.

2. Connect power (+5 V) and ground to the ICs first. Power connections are shown in Fig. 11-6. IMPORTANT: Be sure that your trainer power is off before doing any wiring. Just to be absolutely certain about this, unplug the trainer from the ac line before doing any wiring.

3. Connect the remainder of the circuit as shown in Fig. 11-6. Mark off lines on the logic diagram as you make connections. That helps prevent errors such as skipped or redundant connections. It is also a good idea to color-code the connections. For example, you might make all connections to the data bus with blue wire, all connections to the address bus with white wire, and so on. Doing that helps keep things better organized. It also makes troubleshooting a little easier, should that become necessary.

4. Double-check your wiring, or better yet, have someone else check your wiring while you check his or hers.

5. Turn on your trainer. You should get the usual start-up message. If you don't, turn off the power, unplug the trainer, and recheck your wiring. It takes only one wrong connection to make the system malfunction. If everything appears to be OK, proceed to step 6.

6. Connect the logic probe to +5 V and GND. Hold the probe tip on the $\overline{CS}$ input of U4. Record the probe indication on a separate sheet. Repeat this step for $\overline{CS}$ of U5.

   $\overline{CS}_{U4}$ = _____

   $\overline{CS}_{U5}$ = _____

7. While monitoring $\overline{CS}$ of either U4 or U5 with the logic probe, examine the contents of address 0400_{16}. The logic probe should indicate that a pulse has occurred. The pulse was the assertion of $\overline{CS}$ when the contents of location 0400_{16} were read and transferred into the 6802.

8. Change the contents of location 0400_{16} while monitoring the CS pin of one of the RAMS. A low pulse should occur when you change the contents.

9. Examine the contents of location 0400_{16}. The value entered in step 8 should now be held in this location.

10. Obviously, it would be quite inefficient and time-consuming to manually examine and change each location in the expansion RAM, because there are 1024 locations. Consider that, if you could examine, change, and reexamine the contents of a location every 2 s (you would have to be very fast to do so), it would take you over half an hour to check out 1024 bytes. Of course, here we assume that a simple memory test is being performed. If, for example, you attempted to do the rolling memory test manually, it would take over 6 days without stopping to complete.

```
0000 6F 00 30   CLR [0030]      ;Clear error counter
0003 CE 04 00   LDX# 0400       ;Initialize test RAM pointer
0006 4F         CLRA            ;Clear pattern source
0007 A7 00      STAA [IX+00]    ;Store test pattern
0009 E6 00      LDAB [IX+00]    ;Read test pattern
000B 11         CBA             ;Compare stored and read pattern
000C 26 0F      BNE 1D          ;If not equal, increment error counter
000E 81 FF      CMPA# FF        ;Last pattern tested yet?
0010 27 03      BEQ 15          ;If yes then goto 0015
0012 4C         INCA            ;Increment ACCA to next pattern
0013 20 F2      BRA 07          ;Jump back to 0007 and test again
0015 8C 07 FF   CMPX# 07FF      ;Last RAM location tested?
0018 27 06      BEQ 20          ;If yes then goto 0020
001A 08         INX             ;Increment RAM pointer
001B 20 E9      BRA 06          ;Goto 0006 and test next location
001D 7C 00 30   INC [0030]      ;Increment RAM error counter
0020 7E FC 00   JMP FC00        ;Goto start of monitor ROM (CPU UP)
```

Program Listing 11-5

To speed up the memory test process, let us modify the rolling memory test of Activity 11-2 to test the expansion RAM. The modified program is shown in Listing 11-5. The index register is set to 0400 (the start of expansion RAM), and an offset of 00 is used when the accumulators are loaded with test data in the indexed addressing mode. Even with the high speed of the microprocessor, the rolling memory test still requires almost 10 s to run if no errors are detected. Because of this, when the program is finished, rather than just executing the WAIT instruction, a branch to the monitor ROM is taken. This causes CPU UP to be displayed, giving a visual indication of program termination.

11. Enter and execute the test program of Listing 11-5.
12. Recall that, if a faulty memory location is detected, address 0030_{16} will contain 01_{16} when the program terminates. Check this address to see if your RAM is good. If an error is indicated, replace the RAMs and run the test again. Don't forget to turn off power when modifying circuits!

DISCUSSION TOPICS

1. The memory test program could be modified to increment the error counter and continue testing whenever a bad location is found, rather than stopping whenever the first error occurs. In the case of the 1K expansion RAM, however, it is possible that enough locations could be faulty to give an erroneous sum in the error counter. When would such a condition occur?
2. Assuming an MPU cycle is 1 μs long, using the program of Listing 11-5, approximately how long would it take to test a block of RAM starting at address 0400_{16} and ending at address $0BFF_{16}$?

CHAPTER | 12

Mass Storage

ACTIVITY 12-1
TEST: MASS STORAGE

On a separate sheet of paper, complete the following questions and statements by choosing the most appropriate letter.

1. A physical storage area, such as a floppy disk, is called the storage
   _____.
   a. Drive
   b. Winchester
   c. Medium
   d. Controller

2. Data is encoded on floppy disks by systematic alignment of
   _____.
   a. Electrons
   b. Magnetic domains
   c. Berthold rays
   d. NAND gates

3. One of the earliest types of magnetic mass storage devices was the
   _____.
   a. Bubble memory
   b. Magnetic drum
   c. 3.5-in. floppy disk
   d. Kansas City standard

4. Mass storage that can be accessed by the computer at any time is
   referred to as _____.
   a. On-line mass storage
   b. Off-line mass storage
   c. Random-access mass storage
   d. Backup mass storage

5. In general, one of the most important and necessary characteristics
   of mass storage is _____.
   a. Sequential access
   b. Low-speed access
   c. Low viscosity
   d. Nonvolatility

6. The floppy disk drive's _____ has a very narrow air gap that allows the magnetic coating of the disk to be magnetized.
   a. Stepper motor
   b. Read head
   c. Write head
   d. Domain

7. Parity checking is a simple error detection technique that allows _____ error(s) to be detected.
   a. One
   b. Two or more
   c. An even number of
   d. An odd number of

8. Cyclic redundancy checking (CRC) is a more sophisticated error detection technique that treats data as _____.
   a. Remainders
   b. Coefficients of a polynomial
   c. Instructions
   d. Cyclic checker cones

9. One of the main disadvantages of magnetic tape storage is _____.
   a. Sequential access
   b. Random access
   c. Volatility
   d. CRC error checking must be used

10. Floppy disks and magnetic tape are normally constructed of _____.
    a. A nonmagnetic substrate coated with aluminum
    b. A plastic substrate covered with conductive ink
    c. A Mylar substrate with a thin ferrous coating
    d. Titanium film with a boron nitride coating

11. Magnetic disks are generally divided into concentric rings. These rings are called _____.
    a. Tracks
    b. Grooves
    c. Sectors
    d. Domains

12. Compared to magnetic tape storage, disk-based storage offers this advantage: _____.
    a. Higher storage capacity
    b. Sequential access
    c. Serial access
    d. Fast access

13. Direct memory access (DMA) is often used for disk drive to computer interfacing because it _____.
    a. Provides parallel data transfer
    b. Allows fast transfer of large amounts of data
    c. Is the most inexpensive I/O interfacing technique
    d. Is well suited to CRC checking

14. Theoretically, a hard disk should not experience any wear of the disk surface or read/write head because the head _____.
    a. Flies over the disk surface
    b. Is made of a special wear-resistant alloy
    c. Rotates with the disk
    d. Is not needed in a hard disk drive

15. The start of a given track on a floppy disk is often marked by
_____.
  a. A notch on the corner of the disk jacket
  b. An index hole in the disk
  c. A start bit
  d. None of the above; there is usually no physical mark

16. A floppy disk with a defect, such as a scratch, on the disk surface
would exhibit _____.
  a. Hard errors
  b. Soft errors
  c. Parity errors
  d. Skipping

17. A floppy disk that is exposed to a magnetic field that altered some
of its data would most likely exhibit _____.
  a. Hard errors
  b. Soft errors
  c. Warping of the disk
  d. A head crash

18. A parking cylinder is used _____.
  a. In a floppy disk drive for head positioning
  b. In a floppy disk drive for track 0 identification
  c. In a Winchester disk drive for protection of the heads
  d. In a Winchester disk drive for voice coil drive generation

19. Before it can be used, a new Winchester disk must be _____.
  a. Formatted
  b. Wiped off with a clean cloth
  c. Erased
  d. Magnetized

20. When magnetic tape is used for backup purposes, this type of operation is not necessary: _____.
  a. Reading of the taped data
  b. Writing of data to the tape
  c. Incremental read/write capability
  d. Continuous tape transport

21. A relatively inexpensive tape backup system that is sometimes used
is the _____.
  a. Incremental read/write tape system
  b. CRC checking system
  c. Streaming tape system
  d. Magnetic bubble storage system

22. An optical ROM has the advantage of _____ over conventional
magnetic disk-based storage.
  a. Random access   c. Volatility
  b. Sequential access   d. High storage density

23. Generally speaking, optical data storage devices that have read and
write capability _____.
  a. Have rather low write speeds
  b. Have high write speeds
  c. Are equivalent in access time to the Winchester disk system
  d. Store information on a magnetic film

24. A _____ is required to interface the disk drive or tape drive to the
microcomputer.
  a. Switching supply   c. Soft-sectored disk
  b. Controller   d. File allocation table (FAT)

25. Generally speaking, a disk drive will draw the most current from the power supply when _____.
   a. The head is being stepped across the disk
   b. A track is being written to
   c. A track is being read
   d. The drive is not being accessed

ACTIVITY 12-2
LAB EXPERIMENT:
DISK DRIVE SPEED ADJUSTMENT

PURPOSE

This activity will provide you with the opportunity to inspect the internal disk drive of your microcomputer. You will use a simple ac line-connected neon lamp to determine whether the disk drive is running at the correct speed. If necessary, you will adjust the speed of the disk drive.

MATERIALS

Qty.
1 IBM AT, IBM XT, or a compatible microcomputer with floppy disk drive
1 MS-DOS and DOS supplemental programs or the equivalent
1 Ac line-driven neon light source

INTRODUCTION

The floppy disk drive is possibly the most common mass storage device used today. Disk drives are rather complex but also very reliable, and an occasional cleaning of the heads is the only maintenance necessary.

One of the simpler performance adjustments that can be made on the floppy disk drive is the adjustment of the speed of the drive motor. Usually a floppy disk drive uses a rubber belt to connect a dc motor to a large pulley that turns the floppy disk. On the large pulley are timing marks that are used for speed adjustment purposes. Usually there are two sets of timing marks: one for 60-Hz and the other for 50-Hz operation. In the United States, the frequency of the ac line is 60 Hz; in Europe, it is most commonly 50 Hz. To adjust the speed, a light source that flashes at 50 or 60 Hz is used to illuminate the timing marks, and a potentiometer is so adjusted that the appropriate marks appear to be stationary. (This is a stroboscopic effect similar to that used to adjust the speed of a record turntable or to adjust the timing of an automobile engine.)

In the United States, the 60-Hz light source is easy to build by using a neon lamp and a current-limiting resistor. Connecting the test lamp to the ac line automatically produces a 60-Hz light source. The 60-Hz line frequency is a fairly accurate reference. If fluorescent lighting is used in the lab, the neon lamp circuit might not be necessary, because fluorescent lights tend to flicker slightly at the line frequency. If the flicker is prominent enough, the timing marks may be visible without the neon lamp setup. Your instructor will supply you with the neon light source if it is required.

PROCEDURE

1. With the computer turned off and unplugged from the ac line, insert the DOS disk in drive A and, if a second drive is present, insert another disk in drive B.

2. Remove the top of the cabinet from the computer. Your instructor will show you which screws must be removed to accomplish the removal. Place the cabinet in a secure location that is out of your way.

3. If you are using a PC with dual disk drives, remove the two retaining screws from the right side of drive B. That is shown in Fig. 12-1.

4. If you are using a PC with two disk drives or a single-disk-drive PC, locate the two retaining screws on the left side of drive A. These screws are in the same relative positions as those shown for drive B, except that they are on the left side of drive A. In order to remove the screws, the drive controller card must be removed. Remove the card retaining screw and gently pull the drive controller from the bus. Refer to Fig. 12-1 for card and retaining screw locations. For now, gently lay the controller card on top of the disk drive to get it out of the way. Now you can remove the two screws holding drive A in place.

5. Reinsert the drive controller card into the bus connector. Do not force the card. Gently rock the card and apply pressure until the card is seated. Be sure that the cable is still connected firmly to the end of the controller board.

6. Carefully remove the ribbon cable connectors from the rear edge of the disk drive circuit board. (This applies to both disk drives in dual-disk machines.) Do not remove the smaller brown connectors labeled 8 through 13. Refer to Fig. 12-1. If your machine has only one disk drive, skip to step 10.

7. If your PC has two disk drives, slide drive B forward about an inch and locate the connector labeled P11. Carefully remove P11 from the socket on the disk drive. This connector may be difficult to re-

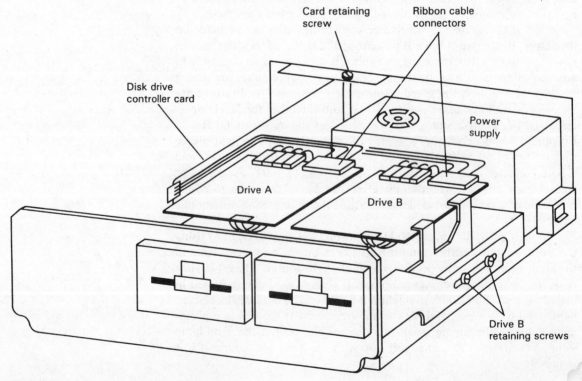

Fig. 12-1

move, so be patient and careful. Refer to Fig. 12-2 for the location of connector P11.

8. Completely remove disk drive B from the system unit and reconnect the ribbon cable connector and connector P11 to the circuit board.

9. Orient drive B on its left side so the timing marks on the bottom of the large drive pulley are easily observed. Proceed to step 10.

10. Slide drive A forward about an inch and carefully remove the connector labeled P10. This connector may be rather difficult to remove, so be patient and careful. Refer to Fig. 12-2 for the location of connector P10.

11. Completely remove drive A from the system unit and reconnect the ribbon cable and connector P10 to the disk drive circuit board. Orient the disk drive so it is on its left side and the timing marks on the large pulley are visible.

    If fluorescent lighting is being used, the timing marks should easily be visible in the following steps. If normal incandescent lighting is in use, your instructor will supply you with a neon lamp to observe the marks with. The neon lamp will operate directly off the 120-V ac line, so be careful with it.

12. Now we must get the disk drives running on command. A short debugger program will be used to run the drive motor(s). Your machine will run just as well in its current partly disassembled condition as it would normally, so insert your DOS disk in drive A and turn on the computer.

13. After your machine has booted up, remove the DOS disk from drive A and insert the supplemental DOS disk. Activate DEBUG now.

14. Assemble the 8088 program shown in Listing 12-1. Use the command A 100 to tell DEBUG to start assembly at hex address 0100.

15. Execute the program by entering the command G. Drive A should be running now. It will continue to run until the space bar is pressed.

16. Observe the timing marks on the large pulley. The appropriate marks (60 Hz for the United States, 50 Hz for Europe) should appear to be stationary. If the timing marks appear to slowly rotate clockwise, the drive is running faster than normal. If the marks appear to rotate counterclockwise, the drive is running too slowly.

17. If the drive speed requires adjustment, a small trimmer potentiometer labeled R_{23} is adjusted with a small screwdriver. Trimpot R_{23} is located on the back of the disk drive as shown in Fig. 12-3. Do not adjust this potentiometer unless the drive speed is incorrect.

```
XXXX:0100    MOV  DX,03F2
XXXX:0103    MOV  AL,1C
XXXX:0105    OUT  DX,AL
XXXX:0106    MOV  AH,0B
XXXX:0108    INT  21
XXXX:010A    CMP  AL,00
XXXX:010C    JE   0100
XXXX:010E    MOV  AL,0C
XXXX:0110    MOV  DX,03F2
XXXX:0113    OUT  DX,AL
XXXX:0114    INT  20
```

Program Listing 12-1

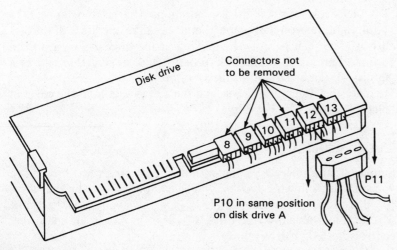

Fig. 12-2

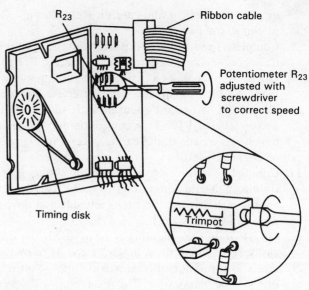

R₂₃

Ribbon cable

Potentiometer R$_{23}$
adjusted with
screwdriver
to correct speed

Trimpot

Timing disk

Fig. 12-3

18. Press the spacebar to stop drive A. If you are using a dual-disk-drive machine, go on to step 19. If you are using a single-drive machine, go to step 23.

19. The speed of drive B will now be checked. To do so, we must change the instruction at address 0103_{16} to MOV AL,25. Enter the command

   A 103

   Now just type

   MOV AL,25

   and hit return twice.

20. Execute the program (enter G). Drive B should now be running.

21. The timing marks should appear to be stationary. Drive speed is again adjusted with R$_{23}$, except, of course, that we now locate R$_{23}$ on drive B. Refer to Fig. 12-3 again for this adjustment.

22. Press the spacebar to stop drive B.

23. Turn off the computer and disconnect the ribbon cable connector(s) and connector(s) P10 (and P11 if you have two drives) from the disk drive(s).

24. Reinstall the disk drive(s). Remember that you must remove the drive controller circuit board from the bus connector in order to get to the drive A retaining screws.

25. Double-check your disk drive connections. If everything appears to be all right, turn on the computer and check the operation of the disk drives. That can be done by looking at the directory of a disk in drive A (enter DIR at the DOS prompt) and the directory of a disk in drive B (enter DIR B: at the DOS prompt).

26. Replace the system unit cover and the screws that hold the cover in place.

DISCUSSION TOPICS

1. Suppose that a microcomputer with dual disk drives was brought to you with the following problem: "The computer boots up, but drive B will not run." Describe a simple way by which you could determine whether the problem was in drive B itself or in the circuit board that controls both disk drives.

2. By using reference materials for your machine, write a BASIC program that will implement the program in Listing 12-1.

CHAPTER 13

Microprocessor I/O

ACTIVITY 13-1
TEST: MICROPROCESSOR I/O

On a separate sheet of paper, choose the answer that best fits the following statements and questions.

1. Data communication protocols could be defined as being _____.
   a. The conductors over which signals are transmitted and received
   b. The engineers that design data communication systems
   c. Devices that communicate with the microcomputer
   d. The rules that govern the organization and flow of data

2. ASCII is considered to be a(n) _____ code.
   a. Numeric
   b. Alphanumeric
   c. Serial
   d. Parallel

3. The transmission of data is often controlled by _____.
   a. Transmission lines
   b. Handshaking lines
   c. EBCDIC interrogators
   d. Address lines

4. A form of data transmission in which the time between data bytes being sent is unknown or unpredictable is called _____.
   a. Synchronous data transmission
   b. Asynchronous data transmission
   c. SDLC data transmission
   d. Bisync data transmission

5. One of the most widely used parallel I/O interfaces is _____.
   a. The IEEE-488
   b. The GBIP
   c. The HPIB
   d. Any of the above

6. A bidirectional parallel port requires the use of _____ bidirectional buffers to interface the data bus with the outside world.
   a. Tristate logic   c. ECL logic
   b. Standard TTL   d. Handshaking

7. The Centronics interface and the SCSI are examples of _____ data communication interfaces.
a. Parallel
b. Serial
c. Optical
d. Encrypted

8. In comparison to parallel data communications schemes, serial data communication techniques are _____, especially over longer distances.
a. Less expensive
b. More expensive
c. More susceptible to noise
d. Not used very often

9. An LSI device that is used to implement serial data communication capability is the _____.
a. LIFO register
b. UART
c. Bus controller
d. Parallel-in parallel-out register

10. The speed of data transmission, in bits per second, is called _____.
a. Refresh clock frequency
b. Scan rate
c. Baud rate
d. Interest rate

11. Parity checking, when used, can detect only _____ percent of all possible errors, and the number of errors must be _____.
a. 50; even
b. 50; odd
c. 50; a multiple of 2
d. 25; a power of 2

12. When a word of data is transmitted in serial format, it is often preceded by a start bit and ended with one or more stop bits. When the start bit is missed or not detected by the receiver for some reason, a(n) _____ error is said to have occurred.
a. Parity
b. Framing
c. CRC
d. Stack overflow

13. Which of the following is not an essential part of a serial data communications receiver or transmitter? _____
a. A serial-in parallel-out shift register
b. A clock
c. A parity check circuit
d. A parallel-in serial-out shift register

14. When 7-bit ASCII code is being sent serially and an 8-bit data word is expected by the receiver, the eighth data bit is usually used _____.
a. For error detection   c. For either of the above
b. As a parity bit   d. For none of the above

15. The typical UART operates from a clock that is independent of the microprocessor. Such operation is called _____.
a. Independent operation   c. Synchronized operation
b. Strobed operation   d. Asynchronous operation

16. The most popular short-haul (50-ft maximum) serial communications standard is _____.
    a. IEEE-488
    b. DB-25
    c. RS-232
    d. EBCDIC

17. A certain modem holds its output line in the marking condition when it is idling. The mark is equivalent to a _____ logic level.
    a. Low
    b. High
    c. Indeterminate
    d. Tristate

18. When two modems can communicate with each other simultaneously, _____ operation is in use.
    a. Half-duplex
    b. Full-duplex
    c. Synchronous
    d. QPSK

19. Many modems use two different frequencies to represent binary data. This method of impressing data onto telephone lines is called _____.
    a. Phase shift keying
    b. MFM
    c. Frequency shift keying
    d. Pulse width modulation

20. Most keyboards are arranged in a square or rectangular grid that is usually called a(n) _____.
    a. Array
    b. Matrix
    c. ROM encoder
    d. Vector transputer

21. Mechanical switches sometimes tend to make and break contact several times when activated. This action is called _____.
    a. Bounce
    b. Scanning
    c. Row decoding
    d. Contact conditioning

22. Terminals may be considered to be smart or dumb. A dumb terminal _____.
    a. Can usually be used to produce graphics
    b. Lacks the features found on smart terminals
    c. Cannot contain a microprocessor
    d. May not be considered to be a VDT

23. A 4-bit D/A converter can produce _____ different voltage levels at its output terminal.
    a. 4
    b. 8
    c. 16
    d. 32

24. The MSB of a certain 3-bit D/A converter has a weight of 5.00 V. What is the output of the converter if all three input bits are high?
    a. 5.00 V
    b. 8.75 V
    c. 10 V
    d. Not enough information is given

25. The _____ type of D/A converter is much more popular than the simple weighted resistor summing amp type D/A converter.
   a. Flash converter
   b. Successive approximation converter
   c. Half-adder converter
   d. R-2R ladder converter

26. During a conversion, the successive approximation register (SAR) A/D converter requires that the input voltage be held constant. This action is accomplished through the use of _____.
   a. A comparator
   b. Glitch latching circuits
   c. Continuous balance algorithms
   d. A sample-and-hold circuit

27. A particular application requires an 8-bit flash converter to be used to meet conversion speed requirements. _____ comparators would be required to realize this circuit.
   a. 8
   b. 64
   c. 255
   d. 256

28. Speech synthesis may be implemented by using any of several techniques. One popular method is to construct words by stringing together basic sounds that make up words. _____ is the name of this speech synthesis technique.
   a. Phoneme synthesis
   b. Linear predictive coding
   c. Digital filtering
   d. Fricative voicing

29. A track ball is an input device that uses the relative rotation of a ball to represent _____.
   a. Analog voltages
   b. Serial data
   c. Pulses
   d. x and y coordinates

30. Joysticks, track balls, and optical encoder disks are all examples of _____.
   a. D/A converters
   b. Transducers
   c. Photodetectors
   d. Parallel I/O devices

ACTIVITY 13-2
LAB EXPERIMENT:
PARALLEL I/O

PURPOSE

This experiment will familiarize you with the design and operation of microprocessor input and output ports. Port control instructions also will be examined.

MATERIALS

Qty.

1   Microprocessor trainer
1   74LS02 quad two-input NOR

2 74LS30 dual eight-input NAND
1 74LS42 decoder
2 74LS75 quad D-latch
1 74LS241 octal line driver/receiver
8 180-Ω $\frac{1}{4}$-W resistors*
8 LEDs*
1 8-bit DIP switch*
1 Dual-trace oscilloscope (10-MHz or greater bandwidth)

*Not required if your trainer has a DIP switch and discrete LEDs built in (the Heath ET-3400 or series similar trainer).

INTRODUCTION

Often you want the microprocessor to interact with the outside world. To do that, you need to get a data word in from the outside world or put a data word out to the outside world. That is done by using the parallel data interface. Usually the parallel data port has the same number of bits as there are in the microprocessor's data word.

Parallel inputs are usually quite simple. The data is usually buffered through a receiver that connects the data to the microprocessor's data bus when it is addressed.

Parallel outputs usually have a latch that holds the data. Once the latch is addressed, a write signal loads the microprocessor data bus's current data word into the latch. This output is held until a new word is latched.

Both parallel inputs and parallel outputs are sometimes supported by status and control registers. The data in these registers simplifies the transfer of data into and out of the microprocessor.

Parallel I/O ports can be either addressed as I/O devices or memory-mapped. The kind of addressing you use depends on the microprocessor, because some microprocessors do not have separate I/O instructions. They, of course, must use memory-mapped I/O.

PROCEDURE

Part 1

1. Carefully study the schematic in Fig. 13-1; it shows a simple parallel input port. The input is constructed with a 74LS241 octal line driver-receiver. In this case it is used to drive the microprocessor's data bus.

   The two 74LS30s, one-fourth of the 74LS02, and the 74LS42 are used to decode the I/O address 3FFF. You can see that this decoder is built to decode one single address.

   The two 74LS30s decode the address XX3FFF, which is detected and which causes the NOR gates' output to go high. The 74LS42 decoder asserts its number 4 output when the valid memory-address line is low and A14 and A15 are 0s.

   If you use I/O addressing with a range of 00 to FF, only one 74LS30 is needed. It is connected to address lines A0 to A5, and its output passes through the one-fourth of the 74LS02, which is wired as an inverter. Address lines A6 and A7 are connected to the 74LS42's A and B inputs. This decoder then detects I/O address 3F.

   The other three-fourths of the 74LS02 is used to generate a READ ENABLE (RE) pulse. This circuit commands the octal line driver-receiver to go from its high-impedance state into an active state. That happens when the proper address is decoded *and* when

91

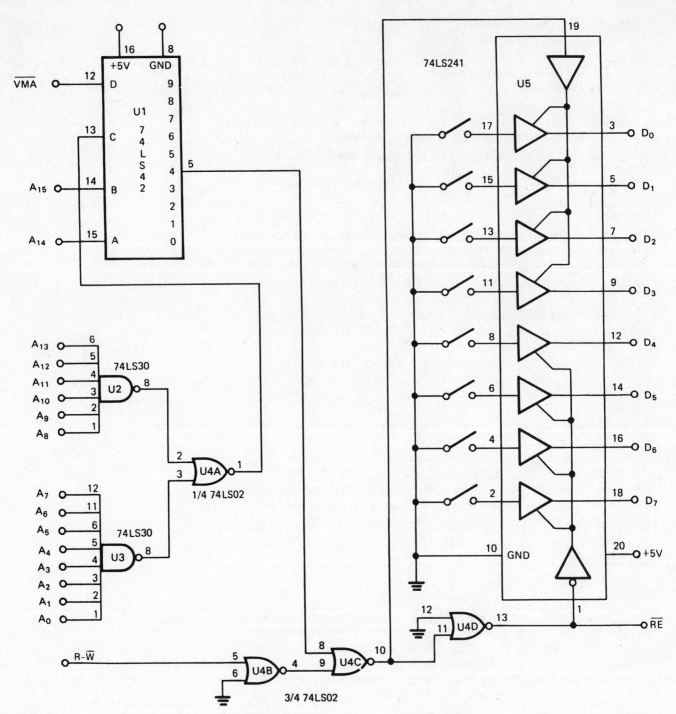

Fig. 13-1

a READ pulse is received. When it is selected, it drives the micro-processor's data bus. Note: If you are using a microprocessor bread-board with separate I/O addressing, this signal will have to be taken from the I/O READ-WRITE (R-$\overline{W}$) line. As you can see, this logic is implemented in NOR gates.

The binary data is generated by an 8-bit DIP switch. Of course, the data can come from any 8-bit TTL source.

2. Turn the microprocessor breadboard off.

3. Install the two 74LS30s, the 74LS02, and the 74LS42. Wire +5 V, GND, the address lines A0 to A15, $\overline{VMA}$, and the decoder NOR gate.

4. Turn on the microprocessor breadboard and key in a short program that loops while addressing 3FFF. For example:

```
0000    B6 3F FF    LDAA[3FFF]  ;Extended
0003    7E 00 00    JMP 0000    ;Extended
```

5. Execute the program first in the single-step mode and then by using the normal mode.

6. Connect one trace of a 10-MHz dual-trace oscilloscope to the 74LS42's pin 5. Trigger on the trace. What does the trace display?

7. Enter and execute the following short program.

```
0000    B6 3F FF    LDAA [3FFF]    ;Extended
0003    B6 7F FF    LDAA [7FFF]    ;Extended
0006    7E 00 00    JMP 0000       ;Extended
```

8. Connect the second trace to the 74LS42's pin 6. What does the display show you? What is being tested?

9. Turn the microprocessor breadboard off.

10. Install the 74LS241 and the 8-bit DIP switch (if your microprocessor breadboard does not have one). Wire +5 V, GND, the $\overline{RE}$ logic, data lines D0 to D7, and the DIP switch to the 74LS241 inputs.

11. Turn off the breadboard's power.

12. Load the extended mode instruction LDAA [3FFF] in memory location 0000.

13. Manually clear the accumulator.

14. Set the DIP switch to 1010 1010.

15. Single-step the instruction.

16. Examine and record the hex and binary contents of the accumulator.
ACCA = _____ $_{16}$ = _____ $_2$

17. Repeat steps 15 and 16 for other DIP switch settings. The settings of the switches should correspond to the contents of the accumulator in each case.

Part 2

1. Study the schematic in Fig. 13-2; it shows a simple parallel output port that drives eight LEDs. The main latch is made up of two 74LS75 quad latches. These devices store the data present on their inputs (D) when the enable lines (G) are logic 1s.

   The decoder is the same one that is used for the parallel input port. Its address is still 3FFF.

   The 74LS75 needs a logic 1 on its enable input to store the data. This logic 1 must be generated by a $\overline{W}$ *and* an $\overline{ADDRESS}$. A two-input NOR gate is used to generate this signal.

   Again, you may need to change this slightly, depending on the signals and addressing you need for your particular microprocessor breadboard.

   The data is displayed on eight LEDs.

2. Turn the microprocessor breadboard off.

3. Install the two 75LS30s, the 74LS02, and the 74LS42. Wire +5 V, GND, the address lines A0 to A15, $\overline{VMA}$, the decoder NOR gate, and the R-$\overline{W}$ select line. Connect the 74LS42's pin 5 output to select the NOR gate input.

4. Turn on the microprocessor breadboard and key in and execute the following program.

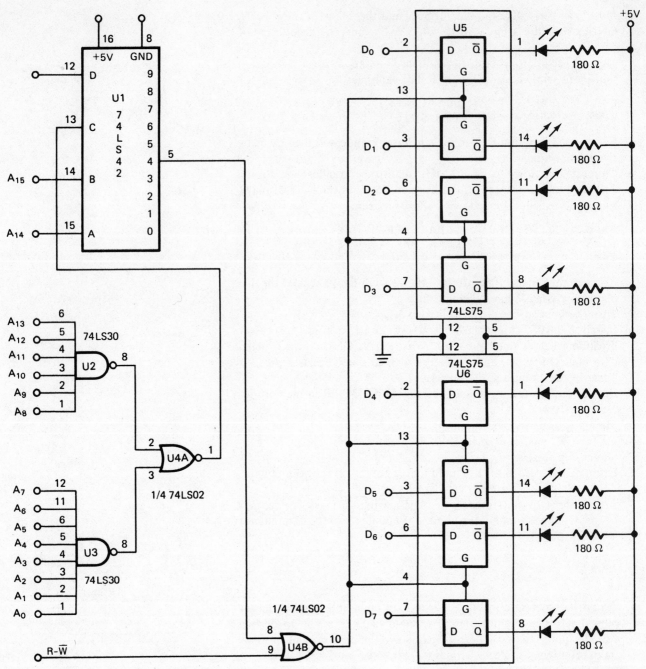

Fig. 13-2

```
0000   B7 3F FF   STAA [3FFF]   ;Extended
0003   B6 3F FF   LDAA [3FFF]   ;Extended
0006   7E 00 00   JMP 0000      ;Extended
```

5. Execute the program first in the single-step mode to test it. Then start it executing in the normal mode.

6. Connect the lower trace of the 10-MHz oscilloscope to the 74LS42's pin 5. Connect the upper trace to the 74LS02's pin 10. Trigger on the lower trace. What do these traces show you?

7. Turn the microprocessor breadboard off.

8. Install the 74LS75s and wire +5 V, ground, the four enables, D0 to D7, and the eight LED-resistor displays. The LEDs are connected

to the 74LS75's $\overline{Q}$ outputs. This is so that a logic 1 at Q makes a logic 0 at $\overline{Q}$ and sinks current to turn on the LEDs. Note: The 74LS75 *does not* use pins 8 and 16 for ground and +5 V, which are on pins 12 and 5, respectively. If the microprocessor breadboard has an LED and LED-driver system, use that and connect the LEDs to the 74LS75's Q outputs.

9. Turn the microprocessor breadboard on.
10. Load the following program into the trainer.

```
0000  86 55       LDAA# 55      ;Load ACCA immediate
0002  B7 3F FF    STAA [3FFF]   ;Store ACCA extended
0005  86 00       LDAA# 00      ;Load ACCA immediate
0007  7E 00 00    JMP 0000      ;Jump back and go again
```

11. This program loads the accumulator with 55_{16} and then sends the value to the port. That turns every other LED on. Next, the accumulator is cleared, and its contents are again sent to the port. This sequence of operations repeats indefinitely. Single-step through the program for a few loops to see if the program works as expected.
12. Execute the program normally.
13. Connect the lower trace of the scope to pin 5 of U1 (the 74LS42). Set the scope to trigger on the signal. Connect the upper trace of the scope to pin 10 of U6 (the second 74LS75, the D_6 output). Sketch the resulting display and describe what is happening.

ACTIVITY 13-3
LAB EXPERIMENT:
SERIAL I/O: USING A UART

PURPOSE

This experiment will familiarize you with the software and hardware that are used in serial I/O operations. A commonly used universal asynchronous receiver/transmitter (UART) will be examined in detail.

MATERIALS

Qty.

1 Microprocessor trainer
2 74LS00 quad two-input NAND
2 74LS42 decoders
1 8251 programmable communications interface
1 LED
1 180-Ω ½-W resistor
1 Dual-trace oscilloscope (10-MHz bandwidth or better)
1 Function generator or audio generator (optional)

INTRODUCTION

As you learned earlier, the microprocessor communicates with the outside world by means of parallel data words. However, when we want to send data over long distances, it is better to send the data serially. That, of course, takes longer, but only one transmission line is needed instead of the many lines needed for parallel data transmission.

To send and receive the serial data, we must use circuits that convert the parallel data to serial data and convert the serial data to parallel data. The shift register is the basic logic element used to do this job.

The shift register can be loaded with parallel data. The register is then clocked (shifted), and the data comes out one bit at a time (one bit for each clock cycle). To convert serial data to parallel data, we reverse the parallel-to-serial converter. The serial data is clocked into the shift register. Once all of the data word is in the register, the data is read from the shift register's parallel outputs.

All the functions needed to perform parallel-to-serial and serial-to-parallel communications have been put into one LSI circuit. This circuit is called a UART (universal asynchronous receiver-transmitter). We say that it is "asynchronous" because there is no definite time relationship (synchronization) from one transmitted data word to another. The serial words are also asynchronous with respect to the microprocessor's clock.

To transmit or receive asynchronous data, the microprocessor software must perform the synchronization, and it does so with a loop. By using the loop, we keep testing the UART's status word until it tells us that the UART is ready to send a word or that it has received a word.

The 8251 is an LSI circuit designed to work with microprocessor systems that need serial communications. The 8251 is called a USART (universal synchronous-asynchronous receiver-transmitter). The 8251 has an additional mode to send synchronous data. In the synchronous mode it sends two special words that synchronize the receiving device. It then sends an uninterrupted block of data words one after the other. These uninterrupted blocks of data are said to be synchronous because the timing from one to the next is known.

The 8251 is designed to work with a microprocessor data bus. It is completely programmable, which means that a mode word is sent down the data bus to the 8251. The mode word, shown in Fig. 13-3, tells the 8251 how it is to function. For example, a mode word of

$$
\underbrace{1 \quad 1}_{\text{2 bits}} \quad \underbrace{1 \quad 1}_{\substack{\text{Even} \\ \text{parity}}} \quad \underbrace{1 \quad 1}_{\text{8 bits}} \quad \underbrace{0 \quad 1}_{\times 1}
$$

or FD_{16}, sets the 8251 up for 2 stop bits, even parity, and 8-bit words with a baud rate equal to the clock rate.

Once the mode word has been sent, the 8251 is set in that mode until a reset is received. Other characteristics can be changed with a command word. The command word is sent after the mode word; it changes the characteristics of the 8251 that you might want to change "on the fly" with your program. The command instruction format is shown in Fig. 13-4. We will use 0010101. This word (15_{16}) resets all error flags and enables the 8251's transmitter and receiver.

Once you have set up the 8251 by using the mode and command words, you can use it to transmit or receive data. As you know, your program will usually loop while it is polling the UART's status word looking for a logic 1 in either the receiver ready (RxRDY) or the transmitter ready (TxRDY) bit. Once you have found a logic 1, you can either send a data word to or receive a data word from the UART.

The 8251 status-word format is shown in Fig. 13-5. As you can see from the command word, the status word, and the pinout (Fig. 13-6), the 8251 is designed to interface with a standard data set (a modem). It uses the EIA RS-232 handshaking signals.

By looking at Fig. 13-6, you can see that most of the 8251's signals are easily understood. We will briefly review them.

- D0 to D7 are the eight bidirectional data, status, command, and mode signals.

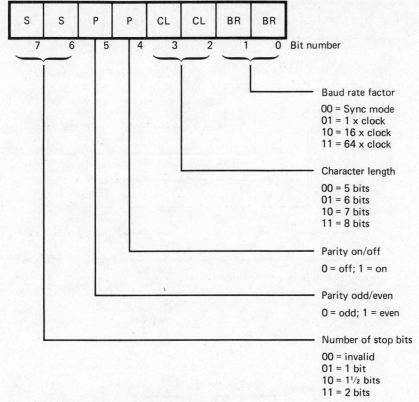

Fig. 13-3 8251 mode word definition.

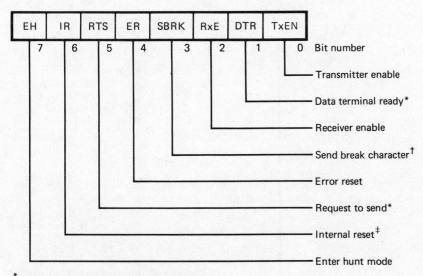

*Logic 1 sets the 8251's outputs to logic 1
†Logic 1 forces TxD low logic 0 normal
‡Logic 1 resets the 8251

Fig. 13-4 8251 Command word definition.

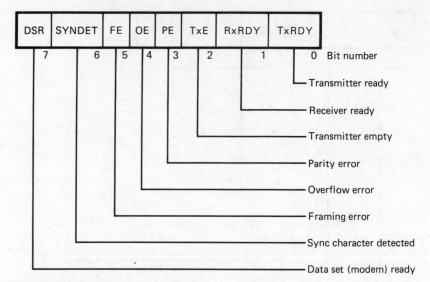

Fig. 13-5   8251 status word definition.

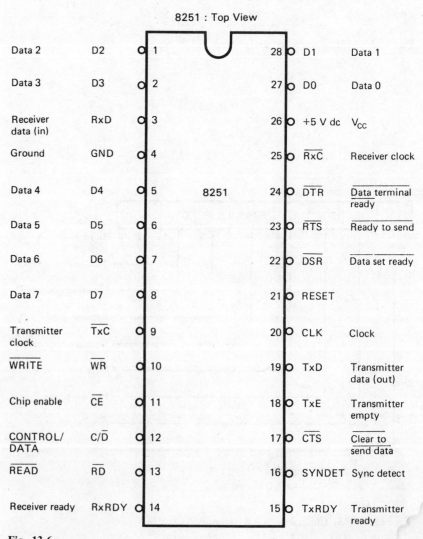

Fig. 13-6

- $\overline{WR}$ is asserted (is low) when you want the microprocessor to write data, command, or mode words *into* the 8251.
- $\overline{RD}$ is asserted (is low) when you want the 8251 to send data or status words to the microprocessor.
- $C/\overline{D}$ is *not* asserted (is high) when you want to tell the 8251 that the word being written is a mode word (the first word after a reset) or a command word. It is also high if you are reading a status word.
- $C/\overline{D}$ *is* asserted when you read or write a data word.
- $\overline{CE}$ must be asserted (the chip must be addressed) before you can write or read.
- $\overline{TxC}$ and $\overline{RxC}$ are $\times 1$, $\times 16$, or $\times 64$ transmitter and receiver clock signals.
- CLK is a high-speed clock for the 8251's internal-logic timing. Usually it comes from the system's $\phi2$ clock. It must be 30 times the transmitter or receiver clock signals' rate.
- RESET clears all the 8251's control and status registers. Once reset, the 8251 *must* be loaded with a new mode word.
- TxD and RxD are the transmitted and received serial data signals.
- $\overline{DTR}$, $\overline{RTS}$, $\overline{DSR}$, and $\overline{CTS}$ are the 8251's control input/outputs used to connect it to a modem's control lines.
- TxE, RxRDY, and TxRDY are outputs that can be used to drive interrupts if a polling technique is not used.

The 8251 sends data 1 bit at a time. First, it sends a start bit. Second, it sends the data bits in the order of LSB first and MSB last. Third, it sends a parity bit as the last data bit, *if parity is enabled*. Fourth, it sends one or two stop bits.

In this experiment, we use two different addresses. One is for data (2400_{16}), and the other is for mode, control, and status (2000_{16}). These two addresses are chosen to simplify the address decoding. You will see that we do not use complete decoding. You may need to do more complete decoding, depending on your microprocessor's memory map.

PROCEDURE

Part 1

1. Examine the flowchart in Fig. 13-7. The first two steps set up the 8251's mode and command words. Next comes a status read. The program then loops until the TxRDY bit is set. When that occurs, the program outputs the data word 55_{16} to the 8251. Note: This program sends the word 55_{16} every chance it gets.

2. The program in Listing 13-1 implements the flowchart in 6802 machine code. If a microprocessor with a separate I/O address space was used (recall that the 6802 uses memory-mapped I/O), then OUT and IN instructions will be used in place of STAA and LDAA instructions when writing to or reading from the 8251. For example, both of the following program fragments write mode word CF_{16} to the

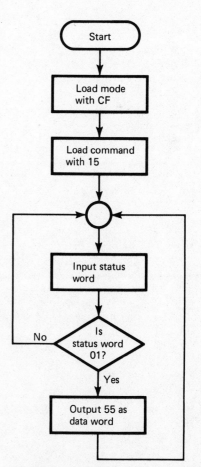

Fig. 13-7. **Sending a data word with the 8251.**

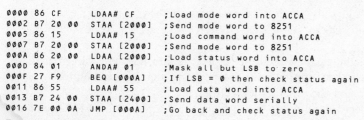

```
0000 86 CF      LDAA# CF      ;Load mode word into ACCA
0002 B7 20 00   STAA [2000]   ;Send mode word to 8251
0005 86 15      LDAA# 15      ;Load command word into ACCA
0007 B7 20 00   STAA [2000]   ;Send mode word to 8251
000A B6 20 00   LDAA [2000]   ;Load status word into ACCA
000D 84 01      ANDA# 01      ;Mask all but LSB to zero
000F 27 F9      BEQ [000A]    ;If LSB = 0 then check status again
0011 86 55      LDAA# 55      ;Load data word into ACCA
0013 B7 24 00   STAA [2400]   ;Send data word serially
0016 7E 00 0A   JMP [000A]    ;Go back and check status again
```

Program Listing 13-1

99

8251 at I/O address 20_{16} (I/O mapped) or address 2000_{16} (memory-mapped I/O). The I/O-mapped version is written in 8088 mnemonics and the memory-mapped version in 6802 mnemonics.

I/O Mapped		Memory Mapped	
Address	Instruction	Address	Instruction
Start	MOV AL,CF OUT 20,AL	Start	LDAA CF STAA 2000

3. Load the program of Listing 13-1. Verify that the program has been entered correctly.

4. Test the program by using the microprocessor's single-step mode. When you input data from the status register, you will get a random number because there is no hardware. Manually enter both cases. Single-step through each one to make sure that the program's loops work properly. Change the addresses so that the instructions address RAM. Also change the IN and OUT intructions to LDA and STA instructions. You can now make sure that the program is writing to RAM and reading from RAM. Run the program, using the microprocessor breadboard's normal mode. Make sure that it runs without halting the processor.

Part 2

1. Carefully study the schematic in Fig. 13-8; it shows one way to connect an 8251 to a microprocessor breadboard. In this schematic the serial port is memory-mapped at 2000_{16} and 2400_{16}. It can be connected to I/O ports 20_{16} and 24_{16} by connecting the decoder inputs to lines A7 through A2.

   Looking at the schematic, you can see that the decoder does not give complete address decoding. For example, the $\overline{CE}$ line is asserted any time an address from 2000 to 2FFF is selected. Likewise, the C/$\overline{D}$ line is asserted (i.e., the 8251 is told to take or to give data) any time an address from 2400 to 24FF is selected.

   Although this approach uses up lots of addresses, most microprocessor breadboards have plenty to spare. That saves a great deal of decoding logic. You will note that the method ensures a $\overline{CE}$ signal when either 2400 or 2000 is selected.

   How would you expand this memory address decoder if you could afford to use only the two addresses 2400 and 2000?

2. Turn the microprocessor breadboard's power off.

3. Insert the 74LS42 decoders in the breadboard and wire $\overline{VMA}$, A15 to A10 (or A7 to A2), +5 V, GND, and the jumper from pin 2 to pin 12.

4. Insert the first 74LS00 and wire to the first decoder, R-$\overline{W}$, and $\overline{RESET}$.

5. Insert the 8251. Remember this is an MOS device. Handle it with care and only when your instructor tells you to. Wire in +5 V, ground, D0 to D7, CLK, RESET, C/$\overline{D}$, $\overline{CE}$, $\overline{WR}$, $\overline{RD}$, TxC, and RxC.

6. Insert the final 74LS00. Wire in TxD and RxD. Be sure that these are wired as noninverting buffers and that one is connected as a driver and the other as a receiver.

7. Connect the data out signal from the 74LS00 to an LED indicator on your microprocessor breadboard. If your microprocessor bread-

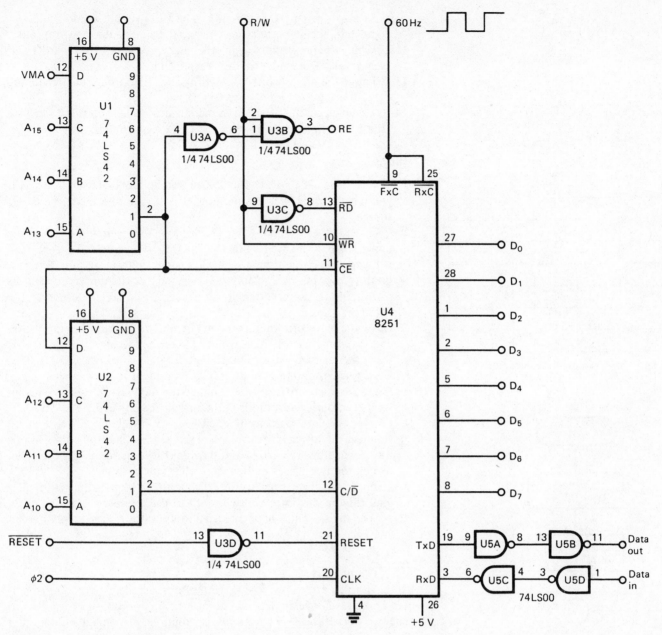

Fig. 13-8. Serial I/O circuit.

board does not have an LED indictor, wire one by using a 180-Ω, ¼-W resistor and an LED as shown in Fig. 13-9.

8. Turn on the microprocessor breadboard. The LED should light to indicate that the 8251 is in a marking (idle) state. If it does not, check your wiring.

9. Load the program from Part 1 and verify it. Make sure that the mode, command, status, and data addresses match your wiring.

10. Single-step the program. After the first step, verify that the accumulator contains CF. After the third step, verify that it contains 15. After the step that loads the accumulator with the status word, examine the accumulator. What status word was loaded? What does it mean?

11. When you single-step the instruction that stores data in the 8251,

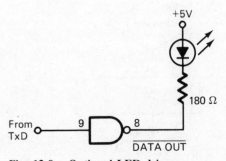

Fig. 13-9. Optional LED driver.

you also start the transmission. The LED should blink, indicating that data is being sent. Can you see the start, data, and stop bits?

12. Execute the program by using the microprocessor breadboard's normal mode. Does the program keep cycling?

13. Change the mode word by resetting the microprocessor breadboard and altering the mode word to CD.

14. Again execute the program in the normal mode. You should just see the LED blinking. Why does the LED seem to blink fast now?

Part 3

1. Connect the 8251's RxC and TxC inputs to a 600-Hz square wave if you have a square-wave generator. If not, continue to use the 60-Hz source.

2. Connect a dual-trace 10-MHz oscilloscope to the circuit. Connect the upper trace to the 8251's pin 15 (TxRDY). Trigger on this trace. You will need to set the time base at 20 ms per division or so if you continue to use the 60-Hz source. Otherwise, set the time base to 2 ms per division. Connect the lower trace to the serial output at the 74LS00.

3. Draw the waveform on a copy of Fig. 13-10. Identify the start, data, and stop portions of the waveform. Are they what you expected?

4. Reset the microprocessor and change the data word from 55_{16} to 05_{16}.

5. Restart the program execution. Can you identify the changed data?

6. Reset the microprocessor and change the mode word to FD. This inserts even parity as a ninth bit. Can you see any change? Why?

7. Change the data word to 07. Can you see any change? Why?

8. Connect the lower trace to the C/D̄ line. Note that the pulses in this waveform are very narrow and may appear to be somewhat unstable. Sketch the two traces and explain what you have seen.

9. Connect the lower trace to the CE line. Note that the pulses are at a high rate on this line. You will need to use a time-base setting of 20 ms per division and high intensity to see both traces. Explain what you sketch.

Part 4

Note: In this part you will work with another student or a team of students who also have an 8251 wired into the microprocessor breadboard. The two microprocessor breadboards should be positioned within 2 to 4 feet of each other.

1. Study the flowchart in Fig. 13-11. You can see that it is almost like the transmitting flowchart in Fig. 13-7. The program loops at the status word while waiting for the RxRDY bit. When that bit goes to logic 1, it means that there is a valid data word in the 8251. You then can load the word into the accumulator.

2. The program in Listing 13-2 implements the flowchart of Fig. 13-11. One lab group will use the transmitting program of Listing 13-1 while the second group uses the receiver program of Listing 13-2.

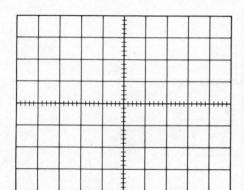

Fig. 13-10.   An oscilloscope graticule.

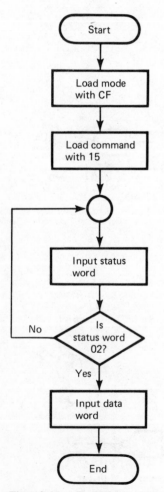

Fig. 13-11.   Receiving a data word with the 8251.

```
0000 86 CF        LDAA# CF       ;Load mode word into ACCA
0002 B7 20 00     STAA [2000]    ;Send mode word to 8251
0005 86 15        LDAA# 15       ;Load command word into ACCA
0007 B7 20 00     STAA [2000]    ;Send mode word to 8251
000A B6 20 00     LDAA [2000]    ;Load status word into ACCA
000D 84 02        ANDA# 02       ;Mask all but bit 1 to zero
000F 27 F9        BEQ [000A]     ;If bit 1 = 0 then check status again
0011 B6 24 00     LDAA [2400]    ;Load received data into ACCA
0014 3E           WAI            ;The end
```

Program Listing 13-2

Make this decision now, but do not enter the program yet, because power will be removed and the programs will be lost.

3. Turn off the trainers and disconnect them from the ac line.

4. WARNING: Connect the grounds of the two microprocessor trainers together. That equalizes current between the trainers and reduces any possible voltage difference between grounds on the trainers to zero. The grounds should always be connected together first if two trainers are being used together. That will prevent destruction of the components.

5. Reapply power to the trainers and turn the trainers on.

6. Connect the 74LS00 noninverting serial output from one of the 8251 systems to the 74LS00 noninverting serial input on the other microprocessor breadboard.

7. Temporarily connect another LED to pin 3 on the receiving 8251. Both 8251s must have the same frequency $\overline{RxC}/\overline{TxC}$ signal. If you are using a source such as the 60-Hz line or a 100-Hz signal from a crystal oscillator, you will be close enough. If you are using a variable-frequency generator, such as a function generator, you must be sure that both are set to nearly the same frequency. Use a frequency meter or the oscilloscope to compare them.

8. Be sure that you have the transmitting program loaded in the transmitting breadboard and the receiving program loaded in the receiving breadboard. The mode word should be CF for both programs. The transmitted data word should be 55.

9. Verify both programs and correct any loading errors.

10. Start the receiver program running by using the microprocessor breadboard's normal mode. What should this program do until a data word is received?

11. Single-step the transmitting program. You should be able to watch both the transmitter and receiver LEDs blink as the start, data, and stop bits are sent.

12. Once the transmitter has started, wait until it has finished transmitting one complete word. How will you know that it is finished? Reset the receiving microprocessor breadboard and examine the accumulator. What does the receiver's accumulator contain?

13. Experiment with transmitting various data words. (Use a different operand in address 11_{16} in Listing 13-1.)

CHAPTER 14

An Introduction to Programming

**ACTIVITY 14-1
TEST: AN INTRODUCTION
TO PROGRAMMING**

On a separate sheet of paper, choose the letter of the answer that best completes the following questions and statements.

1. More English-like instructions that are written to meet a desired programming task are called _____.
   - *a.* Machine code
   - *b.* ASCII code
   - *c.* Source code
   - *d.* Destination code

2. A program that is produced in native machine language for a particular microprocessor is called _____.
   - *a.* Source code
   - *b.* Object code
   - *c.* High-level code
   - *d.* Cyclic redundancy code

3. The process whereby programming errors are hunted down and corrected is called _____.
   - *a.* Object coding
   - *b.* IF-THEN-ELSE programming
   - *c.* Top-down programming
   - *d.* Debugging

4. A(n) _____ is a programming tool that allows microprocessor instruction mnemonics and symbolic addresses and data to be entered into a given microcomputer.
   - *a.* Compiler
   - *b.* Interpreter
   - *c.* Procedure
   - *d.* Assembler

5. Software that is designed in small sections each of which performs a particular function is known as _____ programming.
   - *a.* Bottom-up
   - *b.* Modular
   - *c.* Spaghetti code
   - *d.* Assembly language

6. Artificial additions to a program that allow normal execution to continue even though the program is not complete or certain conditions have not been met are called _____.
   a. Test-negative
   b. ATPs
   c. Data structures
   d. Programming stubs

7. A(n) _____ is a particular sequence of steps or actions that are used to manipulate data.
   a. Array
   b. Algorithm
   c. Data structure
   d. Global variable

8. There are two fundamental elements of any program; they are data and _____.
   a. Arrays
   b. Algorithms
   c. Hardware
   d. Variables

9. Which of the following would be defined as a conditional construct? _____
   a. LET X = 25
   b. LET Y = X + 2
   c. IF A > 2 THEN GOSUB 1000
   d. PRINT "That nutty Schieb pup"

10. _____ is an advantage of pseudo-code.
    a. Inherent software documentation
    b. Pseudo-software
    c. Hexadecimal representation of commands
    d. The sequential construct

11. Which of the following lines of BASIC code will produce Y = 7? _____
    a. LET Y = (6 + 9/3) + 2
    b. LET Y = (6 + 9)/3 + 2
    c. LET Y = 6 + 9 / 3 + 2
    d. None of the above

12. A(n) _____ is a visual device that is used to show how various modules of a program relate to one another.
    a. Algorithm
    b. Data flow diagram
    c. Structure chart
    d. State diagram

13. The _____ construct could easily be used to choose between five different paths of execution in a program.
    a. CASE
    b. IF-THEN
    c. DO-WHILE
    d. DO-OR-ELSE

14. In a flowchart, the decision symbol is used to denote _____.
    a. Unconditional branch points
    b. Conditional branch points
    c. Program termination
    d. Program entry points

ACTIVITY 14-2
LAB EXPERIMENT: DIGITAL–TO–ANALOG CONVERSION

PURPOSE

This experiment will familiarize you with D/A converter operation, interfacing, and software control. The use of BASIC to generate data for look-up table operations will be investigated.

MATERIALS

Qty.

1   Microcomputer (IBM AT, IBM XT, or a compatible machine)
1   BASIC interpreter for PC
1   Microprocessor trainer
1   Oscilloscope
1   DMM
1   Logic probe
2   74LS27 triple three-input NOR
1   74LS30 eight-input NAND
1   74LS373 octal D-latch
1   DAC0808 8-bit D/A converter
1   LM741 op amp
2   4.7-kΩ resistors
1   8.2-kΩ resistor
1   5-kΩ potentiometer
1   10-kΩ potentiometer
1   0.01-μF capacitor

INTRODUCTION

Recall that D/A converters were introduced in Chap. 13 of the text. In this experiment, you will interface a commercial 8-bit D/A converter, the DAC0808, to your microprocessor trainer. This D/A converter will be calibrated and then used as a primitive microprocessor-controlled function generator.

The DAC0808 D/A converter and the associated decoding circuitry are shown in Fig. 14-1. Integrated circuits U1, U2, and U3 fully decode for address 1000_{16}. A 74LS373 octal D-latch, U4, completes the design of the output port. The output of U4 is used to drive D/A converter U5. The DAC0808 produces a negative current (its output acts as a current sink) that is proportional to the value of the binary number applied to its D inputs. This current is converted into a positive voltage that is proportional to the binary input by operational amplifier U6. The 5-kΩ pot, R_4, is used to adjust the gain of the op amp and produce a full-scale output of 10.0 V. Assuming that this adjustment is made, the output of the D/A converter is given by the equation

$$V_0 = 10 \left(\frac{D_7}{2} + \frac{D_6}{4} + \cdots + \frac{D_0}{256} \right)$$

where $D_n = 1$ or 0

D_7 is the MSB of the input word and D_0 is the LSB. Potentiometer R_5 is used to adjust the output of the converter circuitry to 0 V when the input word is 00_{16}. This is called an offset null adjustment.

The circuit of Fig. 14-1 can be used for several applications; an ob-

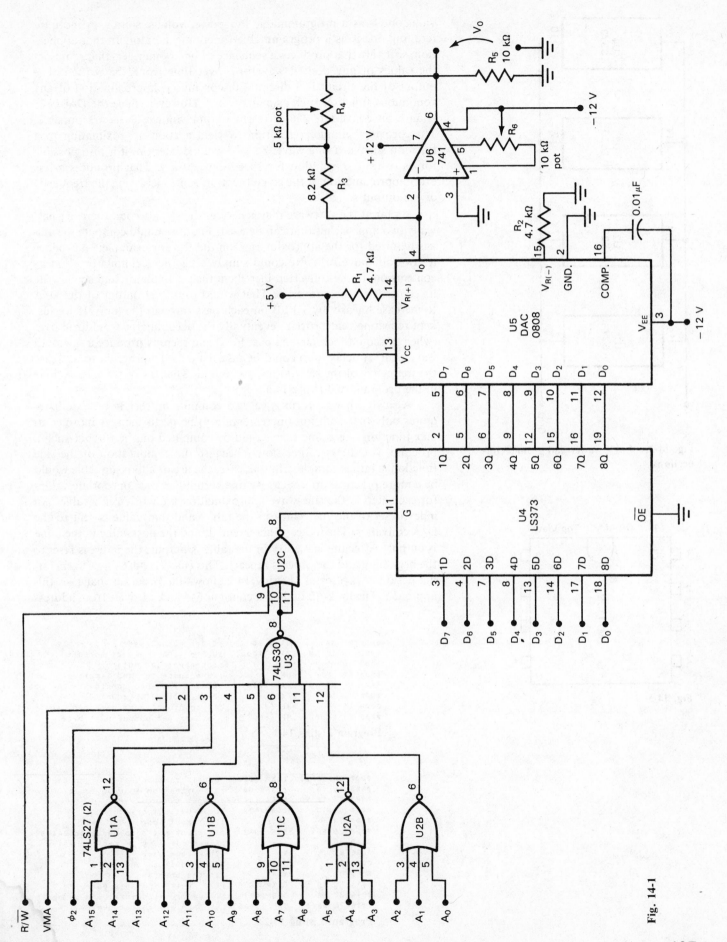

Fig. 14-1

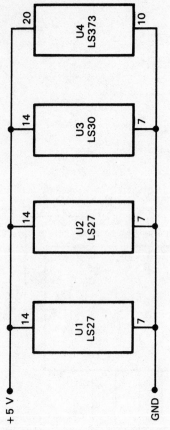

Fig. 14-2. Logic power and ground connections.

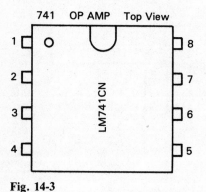

Fig. 14-3

vious one is as a programmable low-power voltage source. A more interesting one is as a programmable function generator. In that application, software that produces a sequence of binary numbers that represent the values of any desired waveform over time would be written. The output of the circuit is a discrete, discontinuous approximation of any continuous function such as a sine wave. However, since the DAC0808 is an 8-bit converter, 256 different output voltage levels are possible. That provides enough resolution to yield a good approximation to a function such as a sine wave. As you will see later on, it is also possible for us to trade resolution for speed if necessary. That produces a less exact approximation of the given function while increasing the frequency of the output signal.

As far as the software that generates the signals goes, there are basically two approaches that can be used. First, we could compute the values required for the approximation on the fly. For example, to produce a sawtooth waveform, we could simply clear the accumulator, send its contents out to the converter, increment the accumulator, and again write its contents to the converter. That would cause the output of the D/A to increase linearly by 1 LSB on each pass through the loop. If we just kept repeating that process, eventually the accumulator would roll over (when the count incremented past FF_{16}) and thereby produce a sawtooth waveform. A delay loop could be inserted into the program to decrease the frequency of the sawtooth if so desired. That is exactly what is done in the program of Listing 14-1.

A sawtooth waveform is easy to compute on the fly because it requires only that addition (incrementation) be performed. A more complex function like a sine wave could be computed on the fly, but such a program would run rather slowly because the computation of the sine function is rather complex. In that case, the use of a look-up table would be a more practical approach. By that technique, the appropriate values for each step in the sine-wave approximation are written in a table. An index is set to the first entry in the table, and that value is sent to the D/A converter. The index is incremented, and the next value in the table is output. After the last entry in the table is output, the index is reset to the beginning and the process repeats. This is a very fast way of generating periodic waveforms. Listing 14-2 shows the program that uses this approach. The look-up table is a contiguous block of bytes from address

```
0000 86 00       LDAA# 00      ;Clear accumulator
0002 B7 10 00    STAA [1000]   ;Write ACCA contents to port
0005 4C          INCA          ;Increment accumulator
0006 01          NOP           ;Save space for modification
0007 CE 00 10    LDX# 0010     ;Load delay loop counter
000A 09          DEX           ;Decrement delay count
000B 26 FD       BNE [0A]      ;If count not zero decrement again
000D 7E 00 02    JMP [0002]    ;Go back and output next byte
```

Program Listing 14-1

```
0000 CE 00 20    LDX# 0020     ;Set IX to start of look-up table
0003 A6 00       LDAA# 00      ;Get byte from look-up table
0005 B7 10 00    STAA [1000]   ;Output byte to port
0008 C6 10       LDAB# 10      ;Load delay loop count
000A 5A          DECB          ;Decrement loop count
000B 26 FD       BNE [0A]      ;If count not zero decrement ACCB
000D 08          INX           ;Increment look-up table pointer
000E 01          NOP           ;Save room here
000F 01          NOP           ;for modifications
0010 01          NOP           ;to the program
0011 8C 00 5F    CPX# 005F     ;Last entry in table output?
0014 27 EA       BEQ [00]      ;If yes reset pointer and go again
0016 7E 00 03    JMP [0003]    ;Go back and output next value
```

Program Listing 14-2

108

0020_{16} to $005F_{16}$. To save space, the contents of the look-up table are not listed here. You will determine the values for the table yourself.

Here's how the values for the sine table are determined: Because we have an 8-bit converter, we could shoot for maximum resolution and divide one cycle of a sine wave into 256 parts. That would require overly tedious data entry, so instead we shall sacrifice some resolution and divide one cycle of a sinusoid into 64 parts. Recall that in one cycle the sine function takes on all values between $+1$ and -1 inclusive. We must scale (multiply) each of the 64 values we picked out by some constant A to produce binary numbers large enough to use the entire range of V_0 possible (10 V). Our converter can only produce positive output voltages. Thus, we must also add a constant offset k to each table entry so that portions of the sinusoid that normally are negative values are actually positive. A little math yields the following useful values for the scaling constant A and the offset k.

$$A = 127 = 7F_{16}$$
$$k = 128 = 80_{16}$$

To spare us the ordeal of writing a machine language program to produce the list of scaled and offset sine values, we shall use BASIC to perform the tedious task. The program in Listing 14-3 does just the trick. You will use it to print a list of hex look-up table values, which you will then enter manually into your microprocessor trainer.

PROCEDURE

Part 1

1. Use the BASIC program in Listing 14-3 to print the list of 64 values to be used in the sine-wave look-up table. If you do not have a printer, the program will give you time to copy the table data down on paper in convenient blocks of 16 values. If you do have a printer, the program will print the list of data for you. The left-hand numbers are the addresses of the data to be entered, based on a table

```
100 INC = .0982
110 CLS
120 INPUT ''Do you have a printer? 0 = No, 1 = Yes'';P
130 CLS
140 IF P = 0 THEN 170
150 IF P = 1 THEN 310
160 GOTO 100
170 C = 0
180 FOR I = 1 TO 64
190 Y = INT (128 + 127 * SIN(T))
200 PRINT HEX$(I+31);'' - '';HEX$(Y)
210 T = T + INC
220 C = C + 1
230 IF C < 16 THEN 290
240 PRINT ''Copy the addresses and data then press a key for next group.''
250 A$ = INKEY$
260 IF A$ = ■■ THEN 250
270 C = 0
280 CLS
290 NEXT I
300 END
310 FOR I = 1 TO 64
320 Y = INT (128 + 127 * SIN(T))
330 LPRINT HEX$(I+31);'' - '';HEX$(Y)
340 T = T + INC
350 NEXT I
360 END
```

Program Listing 14-3

starting address of 0020_{16}. The right-hand numbers are the actual hex data that will be used later in the experiment.

2. Construct the circuit shown in Fig. 14-1. Power-supply connections for the logic ICs are shown in Fig. 14-2. Power-supply connections for the D/A converter and the op amp are shown in Fig. 14-1 only. The circuit interfaces with your 6802 microprocessor trainer.

3. Double-check your wiring and correct any mistakes.

4. Turn on the trainer and connect the logic probe to the appropriate power-supply voltage.

5. Using the logic probe, check the state of the G input of U4. This input should be low. If this pin is high, or shows pulse activity, turn off power and recheck your wiring.

6. Manually change the contents of address 1000_{16} (the output port address) to 00_{16} while monitoring the G pin of U4. A pulse should occur. Note: This is done by examining address 1000_{16} (ignore the displayed value here) and then changing the contents to the desired value. Remember, this is the address of an output port, so reading the port produces meaningless data.

7. Test the status of the inputs to the D/A converter with the logic probe. All inputs should be low.

8. Measure V_0 with the DMM and adjust R_5 so that $V_0 = 0.00$ V.

9. Manually change the contents of address 1000_{16} to 80_{16} and check the status of the inputs to the D/A converter. The MSB should be high, and the remaining bits should be low.

10. The D/A converter is to have a full-scale output voltage (V_{fs}) of 10.00 V, which means that, when 80_{16} ($1000\ 0000_2$) is written to the port, the output of the converter should be 5.00 V ($V_{fs}/2$). Adjust R_4 so that $V_0 = 5.00$ V. The D/A converter is now calibrated.

11. Copy Table 14-1. By using the V_0 equation given in the Introduction, calculate the output voltages that should be produced for the hex inputs listed in Table 14-1. Enter the calculated values in the Theoretical Values column of your copy.

12. By using the manual examine/change operation for the trainer, apply the values listed in the table to the converter and measure and record the resulting output voltages in the Actual Values column of your copy.

Table 14-1

Hex Input Byte	V_0 Theoretical Values	Actual Values
01		
20		
7F		
A0		
AA		
FF		

1. Enter the program in Listing 14-1. This program generates a sawtooth waveform at the output of the D/A converter.

2. Execute the program and observe V_0 on the oscilloscope. Record the frequency of the sawtooth.

   $f =$ _____

3. Experiment with different delay values in the index register. Note the effect that a value has on the output waveform.

4. Change the index register delay word to 0001_{16}.

5. Replace the INCA instruction ($4C_{16}$) at address 0005 with the op code for ADDA# ($8B_{16}$). Replace the NOP (01_{16}) at address 0006 with 08_{16}. These modifications make the program behave as if the accumulator were incremented eight times on each pass through the loop.

6. Execute the modified program and observe V_0 on the scope. The stairstep nature of the sawtooth waveform should now be apparent. Record the frequency of the waveform.

   $f =$ _____

7. Experiment with different operands for the ADDA instruction. Two interesting values are FF_{16}, which has the same effect as decrementing the accumulator (it reverses the symmetry of the sawtooth), and 80_{16}, which produces a square wave.

8. Enter the program of Listing 14-2. After entering the program, enter the sine-wave data that you generated in step 1 (Part 1). This data is entered starting at address 0020_{16}.

9. Execute the program and observe V_0 on the scope. You should see a stairstep approximation of a sine wave. Record the frequency of the signal.

   $f =$ _____

10. Change the operand for the LDAB# delay loop instruction at address 0009_{16} to 01_{16}. That will speed up the program.

11. Execute the program and observe V_0 on the scope. Record the frequency of the signal.

    $f =$ _____

12. We can increase the frequency of V_0 further if we sacrifice some resolution. Replace the NOP instructions at addresses $000E_{16}$ and $000F_{16}$ with two INX instructions.

13. Execute the program. Note that the output voltage is an even less accurate approximation to a sinusoid, but the frequency has increased.

14. Experiment with the program and observe the effects of your modifications. Note: There must be an odd number of INX instructions to get correct program execution. You may wish to verify this for yourself.

DISCUSSION TOPICS

1. Write a program in BASIC that would produce a sine wave at the output of the D/A converter if your trainer had a BASIC interpreter like the PC.

2. Modify the program of Listing 14-1 so that a triangular wave is generated.

CHAPTER | 15

Operating Systems and System Software

ACTIVITY 15-1
TEST: OPERATING SYSTEMS AND
SYSTEM SOFTWARE

On a separate sheet of paper, choose the letter of the answer that best fits the following questions and statements.

1. There are two fundamental classifications of software for computer systems: system software and _____.
   a. Object code
   b. Application software
   c. Compiler software
   d. Source code software

2. System software helps to create a greater degree of _____ for a given machine or system.
   a. Diversity
   b. Obsolescence
   c. Complexity
   d. Standardization

3. A(n) _____ is used on a dedicated system to manage one or more special programs.
   a. Executive
   b. Secretary
   c. TSR
   d. VDT

4. The sequence of module activities is often controlled by a system software program called a(n) _____.
   a. Programming language
   b. Transient program
   c. Scheduler
   d. Programmable controller

5. Upon system startup or reset, the main function of the operating system is to load the _____ part of the operating system into memory.
   a. Resident   c. Multitasking
   b. Transient   d. Memory map

6. The ROM-based software that is responsible for loading the disk-based portion of the operating system is called the _____ software.
   a. MS-DOS
   b. Application
   c. Boot
   d. Directory

7. Instructions to the operating system are read and executed by a(n) _____.
   a. Disk handler
   b. Command line interpreter
   c. Compiler
   d. Interrupt module

8. Which of the following best describes a multitasking system? _____
   a. A multitasking system allows more than one program to be run at a given time.
   b. A multitasking system allows more than one user to appear to have control of the machine at any given time.
   c. A multitasking system is an example of an interpreter.
   d. A multitasking system is an application program that is programmed in ROM.

9. Multitasking systems use the occurrence of a(n) _____ to trigger a change from one task to another.
   a. Significant event
   b. Significant other
   c. Most significant bit
   d. Insignificant situation

10. The CP/M program DDT is most similar to the MS-DOS _____ program.
   a. CHKDSK
   b. FORMAT
   c. DEBUG
   d. EXE2BIN

11. The CP/M operating system was originally designed for _____ machines.
   a. IBM
   b. 8-bit
   c. 16-bit
   d. Cassette tape–based storage

12. MS-DOS was originally developed as a(n) _____ operating system.
   a. 8-bit
   b. Multiuser
   c. Single-tasking
   d. Multitasking

13. The MS-DOS hierarchy of files is called a(n) _____.
   a. CP/M clone
   b. Inverted tree
   c. ROM BIOS
   d. SYSGEN

14. This operating system is both a multiuser and multitasking system. _____
   a. MS-DOS   c. Unix
   b. PC-DOS   d. CP/M

15. An editor is usually used to produce a machine-readable _____.
   a. Interpreter
   b. Object code
   c. Source code
   d. Machine code

16. A(n) _____ is a sequence of characters.
   a. Editor
   b. String
   c. File
   d. Compiler

17. This feature allows a debugger to stop execution of a program at some predefined point.
   a. Breakpoints
   b. Syntax error checkers
   c. PDLs
   d. The fill command

18. A program that accepts as input a file containing machine code mnemonics and produces binary or hex op codes as an output is called a(n) _____.
   a. Editor
   b. Assembler
   c. Interpreter
   d. Linker

19. An instruction to a macro assembler that does not produce executable code is a(n) _____.
   a. Pseudo-op
   b. Pseudo-code
   c. Absolute address
   d. Source code

20. A program that runs on an 8088-based microcomputer but produces machine code for a 6802 microprocessor is an example of a(n) _____.
   a. Cross-assembler
   b. Macro assembler
   c. Xenix operating system
   d. Relocatable loader

21. _____ allow program instructions to be written in an English-like form.
   a. High-level languages
   b. Macro assemblers
   c. Linkers
   d. The MS-DOS interrupt vectors

22. Generally speaking, a BASIC program that is compiled will be _____ compared to the same program run under an interpreter.
   a. Faster in execution
   b. Slower in execution
   c. Executed at the same speed
   d. None of the above

CHAPTER | 16

Servicing Microprocessor-Based Products

ACTIVITY 16-1
TEST: SERVICING
MICROPROCESSOR-BASED
PRODUCTS

On a separate sheet of paper, choose the letter of the answer that best completes the following questions and statements.

1. There are four steps when approaching any service job: understanding the need for service, finding the area of failure, identifying short- and long-term repair options, and _____.
    a. Billing the customer
    b. Receiving payment up front
    c. Accepting a deposit on work to be performed
    d. Implementing a repair

2. Often, a customer's problems are not caused by a malfunctioning piece of equipment or software, but rather the problems may be due to _____.
    a. Inexperience of the machine user
    b. Operator error
    c. Unrealistic expectations on the user's part
    d. All of the above

3. One of the first checks that should be performed when a machine is malfunctioning is _____.
    a. To see if the machine has power
    b. To see if the machine user can pay the bill
    c. To check for software compatibility
    d. All of the above

4. It is possible for a peripheral device such as a _____ to hang and cause a system to crash.
    a. Printer   c. Neither a nor b
    b. x-y plotter   d. Both a and b

5. Most microcomputer power supplies have either _____ or linear voltage regulators.
    a. Nonlinear   c. Liquid-cooled
    b. Three-terminal   d. Switching

6. The power supply of a certain computer produces no output voltage when connected to the computer's circuit board, but when driving an equivalent external load, it produces an output that is within specifications. The most likely location of the problem is _____.
   a. In the power supply module
   b. With the ac line
   c. On the disconnected circuit board
   d. In the software

7. Many _____ cannot be operated under no-load conditions without damage occurring.
   a. Switching regulators
   b. Linear series regulators
   c. TTL logic devices
   d. Disk drives

8. If a microcomputer prints error messages or codes on the CRT, then, if nothing else, you know that _____ is functioning.
   a. The microprocessor
   b. The video RAM
   c. The display driver
   d. All of the above

9. Aside from supply voltage measurements, one of the easiest checks that can be performed at the microprocessor itself is _____.
   a. Testing for proper seating of the chip in the socket
   b. Testing for the presence of the clock signal
   c. Observing for charring or smoking of the chip
   d. All of the above

10. The most convenient way to test RAM is with a(n) _____.
    a. Oscilloscope
    b. Breakout box
    c. CPU-driven diagnostic
    d. Logic probe

11. _____ sometimes require a loopback connector to be used along with the appropriate diagnostic software.
    a. Disk drives
    b. Oscilloscopes
    c. Serial I/O ports
    d. Power supplies

12. A(n) _____ would be required to remove noise from the ac power line if noise-induced errors were occurring in a microcomputer.
    a. Breakout box
    b. Signature analyzer
    c. Oscilloscope
    d. Line filter

13. If you are servicing a microcomputer and the machine will boot up from the floppy disk drive but will not format a new disk, a possible source of the problem could be _____.
    a. The drive controller card
    b. The read/write head
    c. A write-protected disk
    d. All of the above

14. The simplest piece of equipment for detecting the occurrence of short-duration pulses such as latch strobes is the _____.
    a. Oscilloscope   c. DMM
    b. Logic probe   d. Logic analyzer

15. This parameter must be set properly in order for a modem to operate at the correct speed: _____

    a. The baud rate

    b. Handshaking signal protocol

    c. Parity

    d. None of the above

CHAPTER | 17

Developing Microprocessor-Based Products

ACTIVITY 17-1
TEST: DEVELOPING
MICROPROCESSOR-BASED
PRODUCTS

On a separate sheet of paper, choose the letter of the answer that best completes each of the following questions and statements.

1. A _____ engineer is usually given the responsibility of designing the microprocessor-related section(s) of a project.
   a. Software
   b. Digital
   c. Civil
   d. Stationary

2. Typically, an engineering technician assigned to a product development team would be responsible for _____.
   a. Design of the digital sections of the system
   b. Design of the analog circuit sections of the system
   c. Breadboarding and prototyping of circuits
   d. Assigning various personnel to required tasks

3. Engineering will usually send specifications and other materials to _____, who will produce an operators manual for the product.
   a. Technical publishing
   b. Marketing and advertising
   c. Research and development
   d. The secretary

4. Product specifications are developed _____.
   a. First in product development
   b. After a prototype has been completed
   c. By the advertising department
   d. After a product has been marketed

5. After preliminary specifications are produced, a design will usually be represented by _____.
   a. A schematic
   b. A bill of materials
   c. Mechanical drawings showing component placement
   d. A block diagram

6. _____ is a regulatory agency that determines product safety standards in the United States.
   a. Underwriters Laboratories
   b. Dolby Laboratories
   c. CSA
   d. CCITT

7. This construction technique allows circuit modifications to be made rather easily: _____.
   a. Point-to-point wiring
   b. Printed circuit board
   c. Wire wrapping
   d. None of the above

8. This construction technique is well suited to mass production of microprocessor-based products: _____.
   a. Point-to-point wiring
   b. Printed circuit board
   c. Wire wrapping
   d. Solderless breadboard construction

9. Which of the following products would probably not be constructed by using wire wrapping during the prototype design process? _____
   a. A walkie-talkie
   b. A digital alarm clock
   c. A microprocessor-based home security controller
   d. An 8-bit A/D-based data acquisition system

10. Any microprocessor-based product that could emit RF noise must meet _____ requirements.
    a. CSA
    b. UL
    c. FAA
    d. FCC

11. In many companies, product compliance with various government rules and regulations is verified by _____.
    a. The advertising department
    b. The quality assurance department
    c. The accounting department
    d. None of the above

12. The most useful piece of test equipment for observing relative time relationships of several digital signals is the _____.
    a. Oscilloscope
    b. Logic analyzer
    c. Logic probe
    d. Logic pulser

13. A trigger word is used by the logic analyzer to initiate circuit activity storage when _____.
    a. A chip enable line is strobed
    b. The circuit clock makes a transition
    c. The logic analyzer is in the free-running mode
    d. The states of the analyzer inputs match the trigger word

14. Pretriggering is used to allow the logic analyzer to display _____.
    a. Events that occurred after the trigger event
    b. Events that occurred before the trigger event
    c. A state map
    d. ASCII code representations of data